How To Be Happier

Paul Jenner

This book is dedicated to those millions of people all over the world who refuse to do anything to make other people unhappy.

Teach®
Yourself

How To Be Happier

Paul Jenner

First published in UK in 2010 by Hodder Education. This edition published 2015 by Hodder & Stoughton, an Hachette UK company.

First published in US in 2015 by Quercus.

Previously published as *Teach Yourself Happiness*

British Library Cataloguing in Publication Data: a catalogue record for this title is available from the British Library.

Library of Congress Catalog Card Number: on file.

Paperback ISBN 978 1 47361 211 2

eBook ISBN 978 1 47361 212 9

1

The publisher has used its best endeavours to ensure that any website addresses referred to in this book are correct and active at the time of going to press. However, the publisher and the author have no responsibility for the websites and can make no guarantee that a site will remain live or that the content will remain relevant, decent or appropriate.

The publisher has made every effort to mark as such all words which it believes to be trademarks. The publisher should also like to make it clear that the presence of a word in the book, whether marked or unmarked, in no way affects its legal status as a trademark.

Every reasonable effort has been made by the publisher to trace the copyright holders of material in this book. Any errors or omissions should be notified in writing to the publisher, who will endeavour to rectify the situation for any reprints and future editions.

Typeset by Cenveo® Publisher Services.

Printed and bound in Great Britain by CPI Group (UK) Ltd., Croydon CR0 4YY.

John Murray Learning policy is to use papers that are natural, renewable and recyclable products and made from wood grown in sustainable forests. The logging and manufacturing processes are expected to conform to the environmental regulations of the country of origin.

Hodder & Stoughton Ltd
Carmelite House
50 Victoria Embankment
London EC4Y 0DZ
www.hodder.co.uk

Also available
in ebook

Contents

About the Author

Paul Jenner trained as a journalist with the regional newspaper group Westminster Press, later becoming a freelance writer. He is the author of more than 30 books, specializing in personal development and life skills, and has reported from all over the world. He believes in approaching happiness from as many different directions as possible – there is no single technique, he says, that will bring about a breakthrough for everybody.

His other titles include *Beat Your Depression*, *Be More Confident*, *Be Your Own Personality Coach*, *Transform Your Life with NLP*, *Help Yourself to Live Longer* and *Have Great Sex*. His books have been translated into several languages, including French, Spanish, Dutch and German. He has written for national newspapers including *The Daily Telegraph* and *The Observer*. When not working he enjoys hiking, mountain-biking, snowboarding, swimming and sailing. He divides his time between the UK, France and Spain.

He would be delighted to hear from you on his website www.pauljenner.eu.

Acknowledgements

A very special thank you to Victoria Roddam, Sam Richardson and Jonathan Shipley at John Murray Learning, and to those who shared their personal stories with me. I am also very grateful for... oh, so many, many things.

Introduction

Of all the books I've written this is by far the one with the biggest postbag. Many readers tell me they found the book inspiring and that it changed their lives for the better. That's nice to know. However, I've also had letters and emails from people who said they found the book of no value at all. A few were angry and some were even aggressive. I needed to find out why there was this disparity. I needed to know what I could write to make the book more helpful to more people.

So I began asking readers about the way they'd used the book. And I discovered something very interesting. Those who found the book helpful had completed all or most of the practical exercises. Those who found it of no value had completed few, if any, of them. They had simply decided, in advance, that the exercises wouldn't help.

The message is clear. *Do the exercises.*

So I needed to go back another step. I needed to know why some people were willing to try the exercises and some weren't. And I discovered something else interesting. Those who weren't willing to try the exercises approached life in the same way that they approached this book. They were looking for something wrong rather than something right.

In fact, most of us make that mistake to a degree. It's built into our culture. Learning to criticize is part of our education. And as adults we actually pay people to find fault with things. We have theatre critics, film critics, book critics, music critics, food critics, hotel critics and so on. All of this is normal to us.

Normal it may be but it's not the path to greater happiness.

People often challenge me to make them happier. Well, I can't *make* anyone happier. But if I were to give just two pieces of advice they would be these:

- ► First, make a conscious decision to be happier

- ► Second, having committed to that decision, look for things to be grateful for rather than for things to criticize.

Once you do those two things everything else to do with a happier life begins to fall into place.

And that applies to this book as much as anything else. Tackle the exercises in a positive and optimistic frame of mind and be grateful for the ones that work for you, rather than angry at the ones that don't. Keep in mind that their effect is cumulative. I'm not claiming that one single exercise will bring you happiness. It's the effect of all the exercises combined that's the key. Some will have only a tiny effect, others a more significant effect and, in your case, some may have no effect at all. But taken together they become an incredibly powerful force.

So if I haven't changed any of the exercises for this new edition of the book, what have I changed?

Most of all, I've decided to put greater emphasis on *hedonism*. I use the word deliberately, rather than writing 'the pursuit of happiness', specifically because so many people feel that hedonism is wrong. They feel guilty about enjoying themselves too much, especially if that enjoyment comes from physical pleasures. If that includes you, I'll be doing my best to convince you that your attitude is standing in the way of your happiness quite unnecessarily. As long as your pleasure isn't at the expense of someone else's unhappiness (or your own future unhappiness) then go right ahead. Yes, a few rare people may be capable of being happy as hermits living in remote caves with no possessions but that's not the life for you or me. We need reasons to be happy. We don't feel warm for no reason, we don't feel full for no reason and, unlike the guru in the cave, we can't feel happy for no reason. So throughout the book, and especially in Chapter 9, I'll be urging you to do plenty of happy things.

To be a hedonist. For some that might, indeed, mean lots of parties but for others it might equally mean something quite different like reading a book or going for a walk in the countryside. It all depends on you. The important thing is that you shouldn't feel guilty about pursuing your own desires.

I'd be delighted to hear how you get on with your quest for greater happiness. You can email me via my website www.pauljenner.eu

With very best wishes,
Paul Jenner
France, 2015

1

Choosing to be happy

In this chapter you will learn:

- ▶ *how happiness can be learned*
- ▶ *how focused you are on happiness*
- ▶ *how happiness comes from both internal and external sources*
- ▶ *how happiness is the morally right course.*

Do you sincerely want to be happy? That seems like a ridiculous question. Of course you want to be happy! Who doesn't want to be happy? Well, in a moment we'll be finding out how happy you actually are, but it's even more important to know how happy you're willing to be. The answer may surprise you. Let's see.

Self-assessment: Do I want to be happy?

1 You ask someone to do something for you and they forget. It wasn't a life or death situation but their oversight does cause some inconvenience. What do you do?

  a Shrug it off – after all, everyone forgets things now and then.

  b Get angry.

  c Say nothing but seethe inwardly.

2 You're offered a new job at substantially higher money, but it involves a lot of stress, a 90-minute commute each way, and quite a lot of background work at weekends. What do you do?

  a Turn the job down because it will be detrimental to your quality of life.

  b Take the job.

3 You've paid for work at your house and now you discover it was badly done. The builder refuses to accept that there's anything wrong. What do you do?

  a Forget the incompetent builder and call in another builder to fix it.

  b Get a solicitor and take the incompetent builder to court.

4 You've just returned to your brand-new car to find it's been given a small dent. What do you do?

  a Nothing – dents are inevitable and, anyway, there's nothing you can do about it.

  b Cry, because the car is ruined.

  c Get angry.

5 Your boss gives you a rise and you feel pleased. Then you discover a colleague has been given a bigger rise. Now what do you do?

  a Still feel pleased.

  b Go back to the boss and complain.

  c Feel cheated but say nothing.

6 You've just given a speech. Everything went extremely well, except that you made a slip by saying 'a thousand times bigger' rather than 'a hundred times bigger'. How do you feel?

  a Happy – it went as well as anyone has a right to expect, with only one slip.

  b Depressed – I ruined everything by that stupid mistake.

7 You've arranged to meet someone close and they're now half an hour late. What are you thinking?

  a No problem, I'll have another coffee while I'm waiting.

  b Something terrible has happened.

  c She/he's always been inconsiderate.

8 You've been for a job interview and are now waiting to hear the result. How are you feeling?

  a Positive – I have a good chance and even if I don't get the job, the interview will have been useful practice.

  b Depressed – I probably won't get this job or any job.

9 When somebody criticizes you, how do you handle it?

  a Agree with any criticisms that are valid without getting upset.

  b Defend yourself and attack them.

  c Say nothing but resolve to get even when you can.

10 A visitor to your house falls down some steps and is hurt. How do you feel?

  a Sorry they're hurt but not responsible.

  b Guilty, because it was your steps they fell down.

You've probably guessed that a person whose answers are all 'a' has the best chance of happiness. But you may feel that 'a' is often quite unrealistic. Probably you feel you have a right to be angry in certain situations, that you have a duty to your family to earn as much money as possible, that cowboy builders should be taken to court, that being given a smaller rise than a colleague is an insult, that anyone who criticizes you should be attacked back, and so on.

But, remember, we're not interested in how much money you make, or getting even with other people, or any of that stuff. We're interested in happiness. If you didn't score an 'a' most of the time, you're just not focused on happiness, and that's the first thing you have to change.

So let's take a look at some quick happiness boosters. Read through the suggestions below, then try them out.

Try it now: Quick happiness boosters

1 Be grateful. Scribble down ten things you can be grateful for. Look at them and think about them. Remember that no matter how bad the situation seems, there are always these ten reasons (at least) to be grateful.

2 Forgive. Make the decision this minute that you're going to forgive someone against whom you've been harbouring feelings of resentment. Always let go of negative emotions – when you brew poison against someone else, you only end up poisoning yourself.

3 Smile, play and laugh. Turn up the corners of your mouth, wrinkle your nose, raise your cheeks and narrow your eyes. How does it feel? Pretty good, eh! So go and do something completely silly immediately. Throw a paper aeroplane at the nearest person, tickle a friend, roll at your partner's feet like a dog and ask to have your tummy rubbed, or put on some suitably exhilarating music, extend your arms and 'fly' round the room. Anything. Now turn that smile into a laugh. Smiling, playing and laughing (even 'pretend' smiling and laughing) are ways of reducing stress, boosting the immune system and increasing your 'happiness chemicals'.

Key idea: You can learn to be happier

Some people argue that you can't deliberately chase happiness because the things you think will make you happy seldom do in reality. It's quite true that most of us are fairly bad at predicting the things that would give us the greatest happiness. But you can learn how to make yourself warm and how to make yourself cold. You can learn how to make yourself hungry and how to make yourself full. You can learn all manner of things. Why should happiness be any different?

Keep smiling

> Just to remind you to keep smiling you'll find asides like this one throughout the book with jokes relevant to the text. Only some of the jokes are funny. The jokes that aren't funny are there to test your ability to smile through adversity!

Remember this: Choose happiness

We all want to be happy but when it comes to making a choice between happiness and something else, people so often choose the something else. Many people would choose, for example, wealth or power or 'success' over happiness. That's not to say, of course, that you can't be rich, powerful, 'successful' and happy. But when you're faced with a choice then, if you want to be happy, you must choose happiness.

In the film *City Slickers*, an old cowboy played by Jack Palance holds up a gloved finger and tells the impressionable tenderfoot Billy Crystal that the secret of happiness is just one thing. Just one. Naturally, Billy wants to know what the one thing is. Jack gives a mysterious little smile and tells him: 'That's what you've got to figure out.'

In reality, a huge number of things contribute to happiness but if it were all to be condensed into one piece of advice, just one, like Jack Palance's finger, it would have to be that to be happier than you normally are requires conscious dedication to happiness.

So the aim of this chapter is to get you to put happiness above everything else.

Key idea: Decide to be happier

Happiness doesn't, like rain, fall out of the sky in a way that's unconnected with you. Being happier starts with the decision to be happier. Once you make that decision your life will change.

Try it now: Make happiness a priority

Say something along these lines right this minute. 'My happiness is my priority. Whatever situation I am in I will always ask myself: "What is the behaviour that is most likely to make me happy?"'

Case study: Charles

After 25 years of marriage, Charles's wife left him and, the very same week, he lost his job. At home alone with very little money coming in, it would have been, as he put it, 'very easy to be unhappy'. But he made a conscious decision that he wouldn't be. 'I refused to indulge in recriminations, getting even, blame or feeling sorry for myself,' he says. 'I simply refused to be miserable.' Instead, he used his free time to follow a long-held ambition and, bit by bit, planted his large south-facing garden with vines. Every night he took satisfaction in the day's achievements and visualized the successful wine business he'd eventually create. He looked forward to a bright future, not back to a painful past. And, indeed, today he has a small but thriving vineyard and lives very happily with a new partner who shares his passion.

The science of happiness

In the past few years, scientists have spent a lot of time studying happiness. We don't need to concern ourselves too much with the technicalities of what they've found. The key point is that more than half the *variation* in happiness between people appears to be down to things that are either difficult or impossible to change, such as genes, life circumstances (your career and your bank balance, for example) and, amazingly, even the bacteria you had in your gut during the first few weeks of life. Therefore, it makes sense to focus on the remaining 40 per cent or so. And that's mostly what we'll be doing.

Try it now: Start a 'happiness diary'

Here's an interesting thing. If you feel fed up or even depressed you may not be as consistently low as you think you are. When depressed people are asked to keep a 'happiness diary' – keeping a note of every time they feel happy and why – they quite often surprise themselves by filling a page a day. So start a 'happiness diary' today and as you progress through this book, trying out the various ideas, make a note of how well they work for you.

THE HAPPINESS SELF-ASSESSMENT

Fill in this self-assessment now. When you finish the book, do the assessment again and see how much higher on the 'happiness scale' you score. That will be the measure of the book's success. (If you wish, go to www.pauljenner.eu and leave a comment on whether or not the book really did make you happier.)

1 How do you feel most of the time?

    a Extremely depressed

    b Quite depressed

    c Unhappy

    d Neutral

    e Happy

    f Extremely happy

    g Ecstatic

2 How would you assess the frequency of happy feelings?

    a Hardly ever

    b Occasionally

    c A bit less than half the time

    d About half the time

    e A bit more than half the time

    f Most of the time

    g Pretty much all the time

3 How would you assess your baseline happiness (the level you're at when nothing unusually good or bad has happened)?

a Extremely depressed

b Quite depressed

c Unhappy

d Neutral

e Happy

f Extremely happy

g Ecstatic

4 Here we're taking a look at your willingness to be happy. Say whether you a) strongly agree, b) slightly agree, c) neither agree nor disagree, d) slightly disagree, e) strongly disagree.

i I can't really be happy when other people are starving.

ii I can't really be happy when so many animals face extinction.

iii I can't really be happy when global warming threatens the planet.

iv Even if you're rich you should still work and be useful.

v Rich people are often very unhappy.

vi A life of hedonism is futile.

vii You just can't do whatever you want.

viii There's a lot more to life than just having a good time.

ix I'm worried I won't know what to do when I retire.

x Sex should be within marriage.

xi It's wrong to have sex for fun.

xii Sexually transmitted diseases are a punishment for immoral behaviour.

xiii You've got to learn to stick at things and not keep chopping and changing.

xiv It's no good trying to run away from things because you'll find problems wherever you go.

xv Good people will get their reward in the next life.

5 How would you assess the effort you make to be happy?

   a I try to find happiness in everything.

   b I aim to do at least one happy thing every day.

   c I generally leave happiness to chance.

6 How would you assess the amount of exercise you get? How often do you exercise, sweat and get your heart rate up for at least 20 minutes?

   a Hardly ever

   b Now and then

   c Once a week

   d Three times a week

   e Most days

7 How would you assess your eating habits?

   a I eat anything that tastes nice and I'm overweight.

   b I eat anything that tastes nice but I'm the correct weight.

   c I choose my foods on the basis of how healthy they are but I'm overweight.

   d I choose my foods on the basis of how healthy they are and I'm the correct weight.

8 What are your spiritual beliefs?

   a I don't have any spiritual feelings at all.

   b I feel a bit spiritual.

   c I feel very spiritual.

9 How would you assess your relationship if you have one? We are:

    a deeply in love and inseparable.

    b deeply in love but quite independent of one another.

    c in love but it's not really a romance like the movies.

    d fond of one another but a bit bored.

    e unhappy together.

    f at one another's throats.

10 How would you assess your sex life?

    a I have a partner and our sex life together is incredibly good.

    b I have a partner and our sex life together is quite good.

    c I have a partner and our sex life together is satisfactory.

    d I have a partner and our sex life together is not very good.

    e I have a partner and our sex life together is poor.

    f I have a partner and our sex life together is bad.

    g I don't have a regular partner but my sex life is pretty good.

    h I don't have a regular partner so I don't have sex very often.

    i I have no sex life at all.

11 How would you assess your social life?

    a I'm very close to family and/or friends; there's always someone I can depend on.

    b I see family and/or friends quite often but there's no one I feel very close to.

    c I have family and/or friends I see occasionally.

    d I feel a great gulf between myself and everybody else.

12 How would you assess your job, if you have one?

  a I find it very rewarding and look forward to it.

  b I enjoy it some of the time.

  c I need the money and I don't mind the job.

  d I need the money but I'm not very happy at work.

  e I need the money but I hate the job.

  f I'm unemployed.

13 How would you assess your freedom to be yourself?

  a I express myself freely and behave exactly as I want.

  b I express myself fairly freely and behave more or less as I want.

  c I can occasionally express myself freely and occasionally behave as I want.

  d I can't ever express myself freely or behave as I want.

14 Which of the following most closely represents your view?

  a I like everything to correspond perfectly with the way I imagine it should be.

  b I imagine how things might be but I'm quite ready for them to be different.

  c I don't have preconceived ideas; I always find something to be happy about.

15 How do you regard the future?

  a I feel optimistic because I always make sure I have things to look forward to.

  b I don't look forward with any great sense of anticipation but I'm not worried either.

  c I feel apprehensive about the future.

16 How would you assess your self-esteem?

   a I've been very fortunate and done extremely well in life.

   b I've done pretty well but with a few regrets.

   c I know there are plenty of people who have done a lot better than me, but there are also plenty who have done a lot worse.

   d There are plenty of ways in which I could improve and I'm working on that, but I'm satisfied with the way things are going.

   e I feel I haven't achieved much in my life so far, but there's still time.

   f I feel I haven't achieved much in my life, but it doesn't bother me.

   g I feel I haven't achieved much in my life and therefore I'm a failure.

17 How would you assess your charitable feelings?

   a I try hard to make the world a better place.

   b I try hard to help everyone I know.

   c I try hard to help those who are close to me.

   d I may not have done much good but I don't think I've done any harm to anybody or anything either.

   e I just let the world get on as it wants and don't get involved.

   f I try to get what I want and to hell with anyone or anything that gets in my way.

18 How would you assess your self-knowledge?

   a I think my opinion of myself is accurate because it more or less accords with that of other people.

   b Other people think I have an overly high opinion of myself but they're probably jealous.

   c Other people tell me I have too low an opinion of myself.

19 How would you assess your self-love?

 a I love everything about myself.

 b I'm happy as I am and I accept my imperfections.

 c I like myself quite a bit, but I'm working on ways in which I can improve.

 d I hate everything about myself.

20 This final section assesses the vulnerability of your happiness. Read the following statements and then say whether you a) strongly agree, b) slightly agree, c) neither agree nor disagree, d) slightly disagree, e) strongly disagree.

 i My feelings of self-worth greatly depend on other people's opinions of me.

 ii I could never be happy without loving someone and that person loving me.

 iii It's essential to excel at something and have other people admire you for it.

 iv If you're not a perfectionist, you just won't get on in life.

 v If I see that something is right then, obviously, I get angry if other people want to do it differently.

 vi I have a responsibility for the happiness and well-being of people close to me.

 vii My moods are created by the things that happen to me.

YOUR SCORE

Questions 1–3. These are self-explanatory. Score 0 for each a), 100 for each b), 200 for each c), 300 for each d), 400 for each e), 500 for each f) and 600 for each g).

Q1: SCORE NOW...

Q1: SCORE LATER..

Q2: SCORE NOW...

Q2: SCORE LATER..

Q3: SCORE NOW..

Q3: SCORE LATER...

Question 4. Score 0 for an a), 1 for a b), 2 for a c), 3 for a d) and 4 for an e).

Q4: SCORE NOW..

Q4: SCORE LATER...

Interpretation:

0–20. You're never going to allow yourself to be happy. But your high moral tone is based on a misapprehension. You being unhappy doesn't help anybody and, indeed, makes some people's lives worse. It's not immoral to be happy. Read (or re-read) this book and try hard to change your attitudes.

21–40. You're quite often able to be happy but your sense of well-being is frequently destroyed by bad news of various kinds. Of course you should empathize with others but, remember, you being unhappy doesn't help anybody.

41–60. Your happiness is seldom spoiled by the problems other people have. It doesn't mean you don't care. On the contrary, you may care very much – but you've learned that you can help without having to be made unhappy yourself.

Question 5. Score 60 for an a), 30 for a b) and 0 for a c).

Q5: SCORE NOW..

Q5: SCORE LATER...

Interpretation:

60. You have the right attitude in trying to find happiness in everything you do.

30. You're doing a good thing by insisting on at least one happy event in a day, but you're not maximizing your potential happiness. And you're leaving yourself vulnerable if the big thing in your day doesn't work out.

0. Don't leave something as important as happiness to chance.

Question 6. Score 0 for an a), 10 for a b), 20 for a c), 40 for a d) and 60 for an e).

Q6: SCORE NOW..............

Q6: SCORE LATER.............

Interpretation:

Numerous studies have shown beyond any doubt that there's a direct link between exercise and not only health but happiness, too. You should be aiming for 20 minutes of moderate exercise three to five days a week. Exercise literally generates the chemicals that make us feel happy – you'll find full details in Chapter 6.

Warning

Health specialists warn that if you haven't been exercising regularly and have any of the following characteristics you should check with your doctor before beginning an exercise programme:

* over 35 and a smoker
* over 40 and inactive
* diabetic
* at risk of heart disease
* high blood pressure
* high cholesterol
* experience chest pains while exercising
* difficulty breathing during mild exertion.

Question 7. Score 0 for an a), 10 for a b), 30 for a c) and 60 for a d).

Q7: SCORE NOW..

Q7: SCORE LATER..

Interpretation:

Healthy eating promotes happiness in various ways, not least because it provides the raw materials from which 'happiness chemicals' are made. At the same time, it prevents damage to parts of the body that are essential to happiness – you'll find full details in Chapter 4.

Question 8. Score 0 for an a), 20 for a b) and 60 for a c).

Q8: SCORE NOW...

Q8: SCORE LATER..

Interpretation:

If you don't have any spiritual beliefs there's always going to be a little void inside you that you'll never fill, no matter how many things you do to make yourself happy. You'll find full details in Chapter 12.

Question 9. Score 60 for an a), 50 for a b), 30 for a c), 20 for a d), 10 for an e) and 0 for an f).

Q9: SCORE NOW...

Q9: SCORE LATER..

Interpretation:

Close relationships are fundamental to happiness. Married people (or those in enduring partnerships) not only live longer but they're generally more content than people who are single, widowed or divorced. You'll find full details in Chapter 10.

Question 10. Score 60 for an a), 50 for a b), 40 for a c), 20 for a d), 10 for an e), 0 for an f), 30 for a g), 10 for an h) and 0 for an i).

Q10: SCORE NOW...

Q10: SCORE LATER...

Interpretation:

According to some psychologists there's a formula for judging the happiness of any relationship – frequency of sex minus frequency of rows. And a good relationship, as already noted, is vitally important to happiness. But there's more to it than that. Sex generates chemicals that make us feel good. You'll find full details in Chapter 11.

Question 11. Score 60 for an a), 40 for a b), 20 for a c) and 0 for a d).

Q11: SCORE NOW...

Q11: SCORE LATER...

Interpretation:

Family and friends sustain us when the going gets tough and are a source of fun and laughter the rest of the time. You'll find full details in Chapter 10.

Question 12. Score 60 for an a), 40 for a b), 30 for a c), 20 for a d), 10 for an e) and 0 for an f).

Q12: SCORE NOW...

Q12: SCORE LATER...

Interpretation:

You're probably going to spend something like a third of your adult waking hours at work. So job satisfaction is extremely important on that basis alone. But, in addition, work possibly gives such meaning to your life that you'd do it even if you didn't need the money. You'll find full details in Chapter 9.

Question 13. Score 60 for an a), 40 for a b), 20 for a c) and 0 for a d).

Q13: SCORE NOW...

Q13: SCORE LATER...

Interpretation:

It's vital that you should feel free to develop as the person you truly are. You'll never be happy if you're constrained either by your own inhibitions or by the need to conform with what others, wrongly, expect of you. You'll find full details in Chapter 9.

Question 14. Score 0 for an a), 30 for a b) and 60 for a c).

Q14: SCORE NOW...

Q14: SCORE LATER...

Interpretation:

Struggling to create perfect scenarios is almost certain to fail. It means you're trying to impose your needs on other people and the world. Unfortunately, things are always going to go wrong and you're always going to be disappointed. You'll find full details in Chapter 2.

Question 15. Score 60 for an a), 30 for a b) and 0 for a c).

Q15: SCORE NOW...

Q15: SCORE LATER...

Interpretation:

It's essential to have a sense of moving forward in life, to believe that tomorrow will be at least as good as today, if not better, and that progress is being made. You'll find full details in Chapter 9.

Question 16. Score 60 for an a), 50 for a b), 40 for a c), 40 for a d), 30 for an e), 40 for an f) and 0 for a g).

Q16: SCORE NOW...

Q16: SCORE LATER...

Interpretation:

Self-esteem is very important for happiness. Conversely, low self-esteem is linked with depression. For most people, self-esteem is related to achievements. But if you can learn to see your self-worth in other aspects of your life you'll be less vulnerable. You'll find full details in Chapter 2.

Question 17. Score 60 for an a), 60 for a b), 50 for a c), 30 for a d), 20 for an e) and 0 for an f).

Q17: SCORE NOW...

Q17: SCORE LATER...

Interpretation:

Surveys show that people who go out of their way to help others feel happier than other people. You'll find full details in Chapter 12.

Question 18. Score 60 for an a), 30 for a b) and 0 for a c).

Q18: SCORE NOW..

Q18: SCORE LATER..

Interpretation:

Well-balanced people see themselves very much as others see them.

Question 19. Score 60 for an a), 60 for a b), 40 for a c) and 0 for a d).

Q19: SCORE NOW..

Q19: SCORE LATER..

Interpretation:

If you're not fairly happy with yourself then you're just not going to be happy at all. It's that simple. You'll find full details in Chapter 9.

Question 20. Score 0 for each a), 2 for each b), 4 for each c), 6 for each d), 8 for each e) and 10 for each f).

Q20: SCORE NOW..

Q20: SCORE LATER..

0–20. Your happiness is extremely vulnerable to the things life throws at you. You need to work on this, otherwise whatever happiness you manage to develop will always be built on a shaky foundation.

21–45. Like most people you can rise above a certain amount of misfortune, but greater happiness depends on you developing a more resilient baseline.

46–70. Lucky you. You can still be happy in the face of all manner of setbacks. But don't be complacent; keep working on it.

Interpretation:

A low score doesn't automatically mean you'll be unhappy – as long as nothing goes wrong. But the more vulnerable you are (low score) the more easily your happiness will be destroyed when there's a problem. You'll find full details in Chapter 2.

Yes, I'm happy, but...

If you didn't score very highly in the happiness test, it may be that you don't think you deserve to be happy. Maybe you have doubts on moral grounds. Lots of people do. Lots of people add a 'but'. Sometimes it's an identifiable 'but':

▶ but it's difficult when my mother is so ill.

▶ but it's difficult when I know I have to die some day.

▶ but it's difficult when so many people are starving.

At other times it's because something was good but not perfect:

▶ but I'd be even happier if only I could afford such-and-such.

▶ but I'd be even happier if I was doing this with someone I was in love with.

▶ but I'd be even happier if it was just a little sunnier.

For others it's much less definable:

▶ but, I don't know, there always seems to be something lacking.

▶ but there's always an emptiness inside.

▶ but my soul feels alone.

Let's deal with one of those 'buts' straight away – being happy when many others are not.

Is it morally right to be happy?

You want to be happy and yet somewhere inside a little voice is telling you it's wrong to be happy. How can you be happy, the little voice insists, when there are people who are starving?

Well, answer this: are you more likely to help someone else when you're feeling happy, positive and optimistic or when you're feeling miserable, irritable and low?

Undoubtedly you know the answer already. When you're happy you make the people around you happy. In addition, when you're happy you're far more likely to help other people than when you're feeling irritable or depressed. There's plenty of research to confirm it. So there's nothing at all wrong with wanting to be happy. On the contrary, it's the morally right course. Go ahead with a completely clear conscience.

> **Remember this:** Happy people are nice people
>
> Drivers exploding with road rage are not happy people. Robbers are not happy people. Terrorists are not happy people. Happy people are nice people and when you're happy you're also far more likely to be successful in whatever you do.

Everyone is a house with four rooms, a physical, a mental, an emotional and a spiritual. Most of us tend to live in one room most of the time, but unless we go into every room, every day, even if only to keep it aired, we are not a complete person.

Indian proverb

Breakthrough

What was your reaction to those 'Try it now' suggestions I made earlier?

a I have serious problems and they're not going to be helped by facile advice about fooling around and smiling when you don't feel like it.

b I've read all that rubbish before.

c I read the ideas but I didn't actually do any of them and, if I'm honest, I probably won't.

d I followed all the ideas and I do feel happier.

In fact, there were two reasons for giving you those things to try. One was that they work at least a little bit. But, at this stage, the second reason is even more important. If you answered anything other than 'd' then you're still not choosing to be happy. In fact, you're choosing to be unhappy. You're looking for things to criticize. You're being negative when you should be striving to be positive. You haven't made the 'breakthrough' to the right mental attitude. Read through the chapter again and have a good think about it all. Open your mind to the possibility that these things might work and give them all a fair go right to the end of the book. Then be critical, if that's how you feel.

Case study: Jenny

Because of a mild depression, Jenny bought several books on happiness over the course of a year and always with the same result. Rather than getting happier she got angrier. She would start reading but end up hurling the book across the room. None of the writers seemed to understand how serious and insoluble her problems were. And at the time of writing this book Jenny remains mildly depressed. There's no single magic solution for Jenny or anybody. Some of the ideas in this book may seem trivial, some may seem ridiculous and some may seem impossible, but in combination they work if you let them. Jenny didn't even try them.

Focus points

The main points to remember from this chapter are:

* the first step to becoming happier is to decide to become happier.
* you need to work on both 'internal' and 'external' sources of happiness.
* everyone has a baseline level of happiness which is partly determined by genes but it can be raised using the techniques in this book.
* happy people are more likely to help others so it's morally right to be happy.
* don't forget to complete the happiness test above once again after reading this book.

Next step

Think of someone close to you who gives you a nice warm feeling – your partner, for example. Recall something great that person did for you or that you did together. Revel in that happiness. Then recall the details of an occasion when this person did or said something that upset you a lot. Now how do you feel? That's a demonstration of the way thoughts impact on emotions and it's the subject of Chapter 2.

2

Cultivating positive thoughts

In this chapter you will learn:

- ▶ *how your brain can be physically remodelled as a 'happy brain'*
- ▶ *how your thoughts affect your mood*
- ▶ *the ten negative styles of thinking that can spoil your life*
- ▶ *how your basic outlook, formed in infancy, can be changed.*

We can throw stones, complain about them, stumble on them, climb over them, or build with them.

William Arthur Ward (1921–94), American author

'Happy brains' and 'unhappy brains' are not the same. Chemically and structurally they're different. But 'unhappy brains' don't have to stay that way. Your brain is actually 'plastic'. In other words, it can be moulded – much as a muscle can be moulded by the right kind of exercise. And not just when you're an infant. All through your life your brain has the capacity for physical change. It's never too late. Only a very few functions are irrevocably set in childhood. You have it in your power to mould your own brain and make it a 'happy brain'.

So let's begin by finding out what kind of a brain we're dealing with. Right now, is yours a 'happy brain' or an 'unhappy brain'?

Self-assessment: How happy is my brain?

1 You've just bought a new car and you're very happy. As you approach your home you see that your neighbours have also bought a new car and it's far more expensive and luxurious than yours. What are you thinking?

   a Great! I'm very fortunate to have a new car and I'm also pleased for my neighbours.

   b I wish I had my neighbours' car instead of my rubbish – how I hate them.

2 Your grandmother, who is quite wealthy, has always helped you out in times of financial difficulty. Now you ask her for money for a holiday. She gives you barely enough for a week but you were hoping to go away for two. What are you thinking?

   a She's a wonderful woman – I'm so lucky to have a holiday.

   b I wish she'd given me more money.

   c That woman is so mean - she's got plenty of money.

3 You support a political party. How do you feel about the other parties?

    a They have some good ideas but, on balance, my party has the best policies and people.

    b Their policies would be ruinous and their politicians are all either corrupt or stupid.

4 You've been given a particular project to have ready by 9.30 a.m. on Friday. It's now 9.15 a.m. and although everything has been properly and competently done, you're not completely satisfied. What do you do?

    a Confidently hand the project in because you know it's a satisfactory piece of work.

    b Hand the project in but explain you could have done better with more time.

    c Ask for more time.

    d Become hysterical.

5 On a trip abroad a pickpocket steals a little of your cash. What's your reaction?

    a Fortunately that won't spoil my trip – lucky I didn't have everything in my pocket.

    b My whole trip has been absolutely ruined – why am I so unlucky all the time.

6 You've had a routine health check and you're about to be given the results. What are you thinking?

    a I feel fine so I'm sure the results will be normal.

    b I wish I'd never had the damned health check.

    c I just know they've found something awful.

7 You're having your first date with someone who seems to be so successful and attractive that you can't help having feelings of inadequacy. How do you deal with them?

    a Of course it's intimidating to be going out with someone successful and attractive but it's also very nice – and I, too, have desirable qualities.

    b I feel inadequate because I am inadequate.

    c I'm going to call the whole thing off so I won't have to feel inadequate any more.

8 You decide to invest some money in shares and the first one you choose drops 25 per cent within a week. What's your assessment of yourself?

    a That seems to have been a mistake but I'll learn from it.

    b I'm a failure – I can't seem to do anything right.

9 At her request you take a youngster on a fairground ride with you and, although other children of the same age and size are having a great time, she gets hurt. Her mother says you should have taken better care. What's your reaction?

    a Nobody could have foreseen this.

    b Yes, I should have known something like this would happen. I shouldn't have taken her on the ride, I should have known better.

10 Your sister, whom you know to be an alcoholic, has a car accident. What's your assessment of your responsibility?

    a I'm not responsible for the things my sister does.

    b Knowing she's an alcoholic, and having done nothing about it, it's my fault she had that accident.

So how did you score? If you ticked mostly 'a' then you have a 'happy brain'. But if you mostly ticked the other options you have some work to do. Don't worry. That's why you bought this book.

By the way, when you're happy you learn faster – it's a scientific fact. So while you're reading this, keep smiling.

Keep smiling

> Professor Richard Bentall, a psychologist at Liverpool University, has suggested that happiness should be considered pathological (related to or caused by disease) because it is:
>
> associated with irrational thinking
>
> caused by a disturbance of the central nervous system
>
> a frequent side effect of epileptic fits.
>
> If he's right, you're very soon going to be completely mad!

Retraining your mind

If you deliberately think happy thoughts you'll not only feel happier, but the chemicals that are linked to your thoughts will bring about physical changes in your brain.

Let's say your boss tells you you're going to get an unexpected and quite substantial Christmas bonus. You're thrilled. A little later one of your colleagues tells you the size of her Christmas bonus and it's double yours. Now how do you feel?

And yet your circumstances haven't changed. The same bonus that made you happy a couple of hours ago now makes you unhappy.

What has changed is your mental attitude. You were content with the sum you were getting. Now you're not.

This is an illustration of the principle that your happiness has a lot to do with your way of looking at things.

> Your living is determined not so much by what life brings to you as by the attitude you bring to life; not so much by what happens to you as by the way your mind looks at what happens.
>
> John Homer Miller (1722–91), American author

One of the keys to more happiness, then, is to adopt a way of thinking that leads to happiness.

In our little scenario you could storm into the boss's office and demand that you also be given a larger bonus. You might get it. Then again, you might not. Alternatively, you could continue to be miserable with the bonus you have. But if happiness is your aim, all you really have to do is be grateful for what you got.

This idea that happiness comes from controlling your own mind rather than the outside world has long been a teaching of Eastern philosophy. But, relatively recently, it has also become a teaching of modern psychology. In the 1960s, Dr Aaron Beck at the University of Pennsylvania School of Medicine began codifying the different kinds of thinking that lead to happiness and unhappiness. As a result, he developed a system for treating depression and various other mental problems, which he called 'cognitive therapy'.

Let's say you lose your job. These are two possible responses:

1 I'm a failure; I'll never get another job now.

2 I was never really happy there and that was part of the problem; I'll learn from this, move ahead and get a job I really like.

Obviously, if you were to respond as in the first example, you'd be talking yourself into a depression and building a depressed brain. But if you were to respond as in the second example, you'd be much happier – and, incidentally, far more likely to get another job.

Change your surname

Researchers have discovered that surnames affect personality. If yours begins with one of the first letters of the alphabet you're likely to be happier and more confident than if it begins with one of the last letters. Apparently, it's all to do with whether you're one of the first or one of the last to be dealt with whenever there's a queue. So change your name to Aardvark and you should be very happy.

This more positive way of looking at the world is the essence of cognitive therapy (or cognitive behavioural therapy). It's a rather highfalutin title to describe something that, in fact, we all use on ourselves every day. Whenever we try to cajole ourselves into attempting something difficult ('I can do this'), or whenever we try to raise our own spirits ('It's not so bad'), or whenever we try to counter a criticism ('He doesn't know what he's talking about'), we're using cognitive therapy (CT). In other words, we're trying to make ourselves feel better by changing the way we think.

Key idea: The problem of perception

Some people object to CT on the grounds that it implies that problems aren't real but are 'all in the mind'. That's a misunderstanding of CT. Of course CT recognizes that the situation is real. The facts are the facts, but you may be perceiving them in a distorted way and reacting accordingly.

Case study: Jacqui

Jacqui was envied by many of her acquaintances – she didn't really have friends. She had a good job, two lovely daughters who were always near the top of their classes, and although she'd had the trauma of divorce, she was living with a caring, wealthy man in a beautiful house. And yet she seldom seemed to be happy and wasn't much fun to be around. Nothing was ever quite good enough, minor problems were huge dramas, and other people were either incompetent or out to get her. In fact, the only style of negative thinking she didn't suffer from was the belief that she was ever to blame for anything – to her, it was always someone else's fault. Eventually she had a minor breakdown and was initially treated with antidepressants. The medication helped, but when she came off them all the old problems resurfaced. Her partner then paid for a course of cognitive therapy and over the weeks Jacqui learned how to change her mental outlook permanently. Now she's much more relaxed, much more fun, much happier – and has quite a few good friends.

Ten thoughts that can make you unhappy

When you put CT together with philosophy from ancient traditions, such as Taoism and Buddhism, you see a lot of similarities and you end up with a list that looks something like this:

1 Theirs is better (comparing)

2 I want more … and more (greed)

3 If it's not black, it must be white (all-or-nothing)

4 If it's not perfect, it's no good (perfectionism)

5 Why is this always happening to me? (exaggeration)

6 I'm not going to like this (jumping to negative conclusions)

7 I feel it, so it must be true (emotional reasoning)

8 I'm a label; you're a label (labelling)

9 I should do this; you should do that (obligation)

10 If it's wrong, it must be my fault (wrongly taking responsibility)

Now let's take a look at these thoughts in detail.

THEIRS IS BETTER

Let me ask you this. Are you happier when you listen to music on an MP3 player than when you listen to the same music on a CD player? And did the music on the CD player make you happier than listening to it on a tape cassette? And did the cassette make you happier than listening at $33^{1}/_{3}$ rpm? Of course not. It's the music that counts.

Similarly, if you drive to meet friends for coffee, will you enjoy their company more because your mode of transport is a Ferrari as opposed to a Skoda? Of course not, it's the company that counts.

So often we lose sight of the function of the products we buy. Instead, we become obsessed with impressing other people. Quite often the comparisons are false anyway.

Remember this: Advertising creates unhappiness

In some ways, advertising is among the greatest curses of our era. We're encouraged to compare our lifestyles and possessions with the richest people on the planet. We're urged to be dissatisfied unless we have the very latest products, as they do. We're told that only 'the best' will do for us. In short, we're made miserable.

Try it now: No more comparing

1 For the next week:
   ▷ don't look at any advertising
   ▷ don't go window-shopping
   ▷ don't read any magazines depicting celebrities.

2 Save up until you can afford to buy four bottles of red wine in different price categories. Wrap the bottles in newspaper, invite some friends around for a 'blind tasting' and ask them to say which wine they prefer. It's unlikely to be the most expensive.

3 If you insist on comparing then, instead of comparing with people who are wealthier than you, start comparing instead with people who are poorer than you. You'll be much more content – it's been proven in various experiments. If you live in the UK, compare with the:
   ▷ 4.5 million adults who have less than £10 a month to spend after paying essential bills
   ▷ 3 million households that are in debt to high-interest moneylenders

▷ 10.5 million people who can't afford to save, insure their house contents or spend even small amounts on themselves.

If you live in the USA, compare with the:

▷ 15 million or more Americans who live in extreme poverty

▷ 37 million Americans who live below the official poverty line.

If you're in one of those categories, then compare with the:

▷ 25,000 people who die every day from hunger or hunger-related problems

▷ million children who don't have adequate shelter

▷ billion people who live on less than £1/US$1.60 a day.

4 Draw up a table and enter in it some of the possessions which, as a result of comparing, you feel dissatisfied with. Then re-examine them from the perspective of whether or not they actually perform their function. The table might look something like this:

Item	Intended function	Does it perform its function?	Would a new one function better?
CD player	playing music	Yes	no, because what counts is the music
TV	watching TV	Yes	no, because what counts are the programmes
Car	transport	Yes	no, because what counts is where I go

Key idea: No more 'bestliness'

Possibly you're thinking that if you don't compare, you won't get the best or be the best. If so, you're suffering from 'bestliness'. How quickly you've forgotten that you wanted to be happy. That's what you said, anyway. So which is it? Do you want the best gadget or happiness? If you want to be happy, don't compare.

I WANT MORE... AND MORE

If you're the kind of person who always has to have more and more then, by definition, you'll never be happy. Even for Bill Gates there has to be a limit.

Does money buy happiness? Well, there's no doubt that an inability to pay the bills causes unhappiness. And there's no doubt, either, that having insufficient disposable income for a few of life's little pleasures causes unhappiness.

So money can certainly 'cure' some of the causes of unhappiness. But that's not at all the same as saying that money creates happiness. In fact, there's very little evidence for a strong positive effect of wealth on happiness. A person who earns half a million a year isn't ten times happier than a person earning 50,000, nor even twice as happy – maybe, at a pinch, 10 per cent more happy, maybe not at all.

A survey in Britain found that 60 per cent of those in the top social classes ABC1 felt 'very pleased with things yesterday, all or most of the time' compared with 55 per cent for DEs. That's a small difference easily explained by the fact that DEs tend to suffer the negative effects of financial hardship. In fact, in that particular survey, C2s were the happiest, at 62 per cent.

> The wealth required by nature is limited and is easy to procure; but the wealth required by vain ideals extends to infinity.
>
> Epicurus (341–270 BCE), Greek philosopher

A survey in the USA found that the very rich (incomes of more than US$10 million a year) were happy 77 per cent of the time compared with 62 per cent of the time for a control group of other people chosen at random from the same area. That's a more significant difference but, again, some of the controls might have faced financial problems that chipped away at the happiness they otherwise would have felt.

Several studies have shown that when people win large sums of money, they don't become happier in the medium to longer term. Nor are people generally happier in wealthier countries compared with poorer countries. Nor does an increase in national wealth result in more happiness. Americans seem to be no happier now than they were in 1946/7, and considerably less happy than they were in the late 1950s.

So while poverty causes misery, we can dispense with wealth as a significant cause of happiness.

Remember this: Money and happiness

The bottom line is: most of us are never going to be very wealthy so the debate is academic. If you're not rich, you still want to be happy. And you can be. There are other far more important things in life and we'll be looking at these throughout this book.

Try it now: Happiness is free

1 In Chapter 1 I advised you to keep a 'happiness diary'. Hopefully you've done this. Review it now and see where most of your happiness has been coming from. Is it from material possessions or life's inexpensive pleasures?
2 This month, don't buy anything other than necessities and don't use any expensive products (except where you have no alternative). Concentrate on finding happiness in things that are free or inexpensive, such as love, sex, friendship, pets, nature, swimming in the sea or a lake, walking or running, and identifying the stars.

IF IT'S NOT BLACK, IT MUST BE WHITE

This is a style of thinking that keeps life simple but it makes no allowance for reality, which is that between black and white there are infinite shades of grey. It doesn't always cause unhappiness because there's a kind of security in it. But black-and-whiters tend to miss out on a lot. They deny themselves pleasures by saying things like: 'I'm never going to that restaurant again/speaking to him again/going to buy that brand again.'

Most of the time the black-and-white mentality leads to a good deal of misery. Either you're a success or you're a failure. Either you're attractive or you're ugly. Either you're a great raconteur or you're a bore. And since nobody is in the top drawer in every category, anyone with this outlook is going to feel despondent a lot of the time.

Try it now: Look for the grey

Examine the record of the politician you hate the most. You might like to buy a biography or research him or her on the Internet. Then write down the following things:

* the factors in the politician's early life that influenced his or her outlook
* six things the politician has done that you agree with
* something about the politician that you like.

Ask yourself: Do I feel happier as a result?

Now try a similar exercise on yourself. Think of something at which you've always considered yourself a complete failure, completely black (I'm hopeless at my job/conversation/attracting the opposite sex). Then write down the following things:

* the amount of training you've received
* the amount of effort you've made
* any examples of where you came somewhere between failure and success.

Ask yourself this: Is it really all black or a shade of grey?

IF IT'S NOT PERFECT, IT'S NO GOOD

You have desirable qualities if you're conscientious, meticulous and painstaking. In many jobs these are essential. But perfectionism is something different. It's striving for a level so unrealistically high that you're either so intimidated you can't even begin or you're reluctant ever to pronounce something 'finished'. However commendable the attitude, it has no practical use. You just end up making yourself unhappy along with everybody else you're involved with.

You may believe, as so many do, that perfection does exist. But I'm going to prove to you that, in terms of the things human beings do, it doesn't. Oh, if I ask you two plus two and you answer four, then, yes, that's the perfect answer. But let's look at things that are a little more complicated.

The test is this: if something is perfect, it's incapable of improvement. So let's take a look around. Let's take your TV. Is the picture quality so good it could never be improved? Obviously not. Could your car be more durable, quieter, more fuel efficient? Obviously, it could. Have you ever seen a film in which every line of dialogue was convincing, every gesture accurate, every camera angle satisfying and the plot always clear? No. I won't go on. When you think about it, you'll see that perfection of that kind doesn't exist.

Obviously you have ideals of some sort. And it's important that you do. But, very often, ideals also involve a concept of perfection that's impossible to attain. Never give yourself a hard time because you fall short of those kinds of ideals. (And don't give anybody else a hard time either because they fall short of your ideals.) Rather, congratulate yourself when you move closer to your ideals. Or, better still, set yourself ideals that are realistic.

Here's a thought. Have you ever been to a dog show? And been mystified as to why one dog is proclaimed almost perfect while another lovely dog is eliminated? Think about it. It's to do with artificial rules invented by people. Change the rules and the losing dog becomes the winner: becomes 'perfect'.

Possibly you fear that if you don't deliver perfection you'll get the sack. I've got news for you. If you think you've been delivering perfection up till now you're mistaken. But, of course, you didn't really think that, did you? No human being ever delivers perfection. But by striving for perfection and thinking you must achieve perfection, you're creating a barrier. In my profession we call it 'writers' block'. It's when you're so anxious to create a masterpiece that you can't actually function at all. Believe me, the people who pay you are going to be far happier if you produce three pieces of competent work rather than one piece of 'perfect' work.

Try it now: Good but not perfect

1 Whatever you have to do today, set out to do it to a good and competent standard but not to perfection. At the end of the day, work out how much you got through compared with a perfectionist day.

2 Try coming at the situation from a completely different tack. Try to see that things you've been dismissing as imperfect are, in fact, fine in their way. For example, take a look at yourself in the mirror. Too short at 5 feet 2 inches? Who says? In fact, you're a fine example of a person of 5 feet 2 inches. Too many freckles? Who says? In fact, you're a fine example of freckles. Bald? You're a fine example of baldness.

WHY IS THIS ALWAYS HAPPENING TO ME?

Most of us focus far too much on the negative and, what's more, exaggerate the significance of anything that goes wrong. We get angry and allow our emotions to build and cloud our judgement.

The whole thing is summed up in that well-known phrase: 'Why is this always happening to me?'

You know the kind of thing. You get bird-droppings on your clothes and you say it. You get a puncture and you say it. You get a parking ticket and you say it. And yet it's never true. You get a parking ticket once a year, bird-droppings on your clothes once in five years and a puncture once a decade.

Remember this: Eliminate the negative

What makes you notice the bad things is not that they always happen, but that they happen so seldom. In fact, if they always happened you wouldn't bother to mention the subject.

Try it now: Accentuate the positive

Instead of focusing on the negative, try focusing on the positive for a change. Let's start with you. What are your good points? I want you to write them down. You don't have to be 'world class' in any of them to add them to your list. Here are some suggestions to get you going:

✳ I don't deliberately harm anybody else.

✳ I always make time for my friends when they have problems.

✳ I'm quite good at telling jokes and making people laugh.

✳ I don't make a fuss when things go wrong.

✳ I'm good at drawing.

✳ Dogs like me.

Now make your own list.

If you really can't think of anything, you're being too hard on yourself. In fact, if your sheet of paper is blank or with only a couple of points written down, we don't have to look very far for one of the sources of your unhappiness. You don't like yourself enough. You don't love yourself enough. Well, you should. For a start, you're certainly modest. So put that down. You're obviously sensitive. So put that down. You're also introspective. Add that to the list. That's three useful qualities already. Many unhappy people simply demand too much of themselves and those around them, too. We're all human beings – animals, in fact – with enormous limitations. You're going to have to learn to accept that about yourself and your fellow man and woman. Just do your best. Nobody can ask more. Now get back to the list and don't stop until you've got at least 20 things written down.

Keep smiling

> Optimist: My glass is half full.
>
> Pessimist: My glass is half empty.
>
> Management consultant: Looks like we've got twice as much glass as we need here.

When you've finished writing about yourself, make a list of all the good points about your partner. Again, here are some suggestions to get you going:

► He/she seldom gets angry.

► He/she never spends money without discussing it with me first.

► He/she is always very considerate towards my parents.

► He/she looks after me when I'm ill.

► He/she likes many of the same things I do.

▶ He/she makes me laugh.

▶ He/she cooks beautiful meals for me.

And then do the same for your children, your parents and anyone else you're close to.

If you really can't think of anything, then it's not just a question of being too hard on the people around you. There's obviously some kind of deep resentment at work, because everybody has good qualities even if they have a few bad ones too. And you're going to have to discharge that resentment. We'll be taking a deeper look at your relationships later in the book.

Next, you're going to make a list of all the good things in your life. For example:

▶ I'm in good health.

▶ I have somewhere nice to live.

▶ I never have to go hungry.

▶ I have many friends.

Now make your list. Begin with your body. If it works pretty much as it should then that's already something to be very happy about. Can you see? Can you hear? Can you touch things? Can you taste things? Can you smell them? Can you remember things? Can you run? Can you swim? Can you make love? This is going to be a pretty long list.

Nobody's list should – could – be short. If yours is, then you've got to learn to appreciate things more than you do. You're taking far too much for granted. You've got to learn to stop comparing with the ultimate – the richest person, the biggest house, the strongest athlete, the most beautiful face – and try to get a bit more perspective. Don't forget there are also people who have almost nothing to eat, who don't have any kind of house and who combat severe disabilities.

When you've finished your lists, copy them out very clearly onto some card or, if you have a computer, print them. Also make the 'highlights' into a portable version you can keep in your wallet or handbag. Make sure you always have copies close to hand. Here's what you do.

- When you get up in the morning, read the lists.

- When you're having lunch, read the lists.

- Just before you go to sleep, read the lists.

- Any time you're feeling unhappy or cross with your partner or people close to you, read the lists.

Remember this: Lists work

It probably sounds a rather silly idea to make lists of positive things, but it's been proven to work in many experiments. In fact, it's an extremely powerful technique for achieving happiness. So do try it. And not just for a day. It's going to take your brain some time to rewire itself with this new and more positive way of looking at the world. Try it for at least a month.

I'M NOT GOING TO LIKE THIS

Your partner is late. You look at your watch and begin to get angry. A little while later your anger starts to become overlaid by concern. 'He's had an accident.' 'She's been abducted.' You're worried and very unhappy.

After an hour your partner arrives. What happened? It turns out to have been nothing more than a simple misunderstanding over the time. One of you thought you'd agreed on eight o'clock, the other nine o'clock.

These kinds of situations happen. The people whispering in the corner, who – you convince yourself – are saying bad things about you. The boss who doesn't greet you in the usual cheerful way because – you convince yourself – he's about to reprimand you. The medical test which – you convince yourself – is bound to have found a life-threatening condition.

In the same vein, we all also like to have a go at predicting the future and enjoy saying 'I told you so' when our forecasts turn out to be right. And the predictions are usually negative. But we tend to forget the occasions when we were wrong. If you're someone who always has a negative view of things, you may be surprised how many times that happens. Let's find out.

Try it now: Believe the best

Carry a notebook with you for the next week. Every time a negative prediction comes into your mind, write it down. Things like:

* I'm never going to be able to do this.
* He's going to cause trouble for me.
* She isn't going to like me.
* They look very suspicious.
* There's no way out of this.
* It can only mean something terrible has happened.

When the outcome of the situation is known, write it in your notebook. At the end of the week, tot up how many times your negative predictions turned out to be right and how many wrong. You'll almost certainly find the latter outweigh the former by a considerable margin. That's an awful lot of anxiety over nothing. Now try writing down positive predictions and see how many times they come true. Yes, more often than you think!

Once you've done the exercise, you'll know your negative outlook just isn't in accordance with reality. You're wasting a lot of energy and making yourself unhappy quite needlessly. Look at it this way. What have you got to lose by adopting a positive stance? 'The people in the corner are discussing their sex lives.' 'The boss is preoccupied.' 'The results of my medical test will be fine.' Of course there are occasions when it would be prudent to take some action, but you can still do that without having to visualize worst-case scenarios. Believe the best until you have reason to know otherwise.

I FEEL IT, SO IT MUST BE TRUE

The ugly duckling that becomes a swan is an old, old story. The duckling feels ugly (usually because of things others have said) and comes to believe this must be true. And so it can be with many other emotions. You feel like a failure and conclude that you are a failure. You feel nobody likes you and conclude that you're unlovable. You feel you can't cope and conclude you're a bad parent. But your feelings can be wrong. You're sure to be far more of a swan than you realize.

Try it now: Be objective

Next time you feel the kinds of emotions that undermine your self-esteem, write them down. Then try to analyse the situation objectively. If you can't, enlist the help of a friend. Write down six reasons why your emotion wasn't justified.

It may be that you're a very intuitive person and don't think your intuitions should be ignored. I agree. But this is something different. We're concerned here with emotions about yourself that simply aren't justified.

I'M A LABEL; YOU'RE A LABEL

As with the black-and-white approach, labels can make life simpler. I'm a loser. He's an idiot. She's stupid. They're unbeatable. Once the label has been decided, there's no need to look any more deeply or keep the situation under review. And that's exactly why labelling is a disaster. It's far too simplistic, takes no account of change and, worst of all, is self-fulfilling.

For example, when you go to play the tennis partners who are 'unbeatable', you'll have given up before even hitting the first ball. When you decide you're a 'loser', you won't even try any more. And when you treat other people as 'idiots' you don't give them the opportunity to tackle problems and grow.

> The only person who acts sensibly is my tailor. He takes my measure anew every time he sees me. Everyone else goes by their old measurements.
>
> George Bernard Shaw (1836–1950), Irish dramatist

Try it now: Labels are liabilities

1 Write down the names of all the people to whom you've attributed labels. Include yourself, if you've given yourself a label. Next to the names, write the label. Now, in each case find six reasons why the label is inappropriate.
2 Choose a subject at which you've labelled yourself a failure and given up trying (I can't dance/play tennis/do maths, or whatever). Then take lessons from a properly qualified teacher. You may not be the best, but you'll discover that you're certainly not a 'failure' either.

I SHOULD DO THIS; YOU SHOULD DO THAT

We all have a little voice within telling us what we 'should' do. (And quite often it's reinforced by someone else's voice, too.) I should cut the grass, even though it's only an inch long. I should clean the house, even though I did it last week. I should go to Bill and Sheila's party, even though we have nothing in common. And when you don't do what you should, you feel guilt. Guilt is a very unpleasant emotion to have to deal with and I'll have more to say about it in Chapter 3. Yes, sometimes there just are things you've 'got' to do whether you like it or not. But far fewer than you think. Focus on happiness, not 'should'.

Maybe you also direct 'should statements' at others. You should smarten yourself up a bit. You should go to the funeral. You should get a better job. If the people you're directing the statements at don't take any notice, you end up feeling frustrated and resentful.

Try it now: No more 'shoulds'

For the next week, banish all 'shoulds' and see what happens. Each time you're faced with a 'should situation', apply a different mindset to it: 'Taking all things into account, will I be happier if I do this or if I don't?' As regards other people, ask yourself this: 'What right have I got to tell someone else what to do?'

IF IT'S WRONG, IT MUST BE MY FAULT

Accepting responsibility for things that aren't your responsibility is a common error, particularly among women.

Women are the nurturing sex so it's understandable that they react this way more often than men do.

Let's say that your elderly father insists on driving. He hasn't had an accident yet, but you're convinced it's only a matter of time – and not very much time. You feel it's your responsibility to tell him to sell the car. You lie awake at night worrying about how to persuade him – and how he'll manage without it. You're unhappy.

But let's look at the facts. Your father is an adult, with more experience than you have, and makes his own decisions.

He hasn't had an accident, which probably means he's acknowledged his limitations and drives accordingly. The police haven't interfered. His doctor hasn't interfered. So why should you?

Try it now: Stop taking the blame

Make a checklist of 25 things involving other people that you consider yourself to be responsible for (for example, checking that your partner is 'correctly' dressed, ironing his shirts, doing the kids' homework for them). Then go through the list asking yourself:

* Am I really responsible for this?
* Why can't the other person do this for himself/herself?
* In what way am I so superior that only I can do this?
* In what way is the other person so inferior as to be incapable of doing this?

Of course, when you love someone there's a natural desire to intervene – and, sometimes, that's the right thing to do. But you can easily go too far. You're going to have to accept that there are things beyond your control and that other people have free will and ideas of their own. Quite possibly you like the feeling that other people can't do without you and that you're indispensable. That's not a terrible thing. The problem comes when you start to worry and make yourself unhappy over something that really isn't your responsibility.

Key idea: Talk to your inner voice

We all have an inner voice, almost like an independent person living inside us. When that inner voice is critical, it tends to make us unhappy and demoralized. Perhaps it says: 'You idiot, you're always doing stupid things like that'. You know the kind of thing. Try talking back to the voice just as if it were another person. It's not a sign of madness. Ask it: 'Why are you saying things like that when they aren't justified?'. Question it: 'What are you hoping to achieve by being so critical?' Debate with it: 'Wouldn't it be more helpful to congratulate me when I do well?' Aim to convert your inner voice, over time, into one that's more positive, optimistic and cheerful.

Resilience

Resilience is the ability to bounce back from adversity. If you've got the 'bounce' you're going to be much happier than someone who hasn't because, no matter how carefully you live your life, problems are inevitable. How well you deal with adverse events is partly down to the physical make-up of your body, that's to say your autonomic, endocrine and immune systems. That aspect of resilience was determined when you were conceived and you can only do so much about it, through, for example, physical exercise (see Chapter 5). Another part may have been determined from watching your parents. If, while you were growing up, you saw them go to pieces in the face of adversity then you weren't set a very good example. Fortunately, you can do a great deal about the remaining part, the mental part, and that's what counts for the most.

Remember this: Happy is healthy

Here's something astonishing. A study of 99 Harvard graduates found that the way they thought about adverse events at age 25 predicted their health 35 years later at age 60. Those who had blamed themselves whenever things didn't go well ended up with more health problems than those who had been more easy-going and optimistic. So we're talking about something very powerful here that has physical as well as psychological effects.

Key idea: Keep bouncing

Martin Seligman, co-founder of the field of positive psychology, discovered through experiments that about two-thirds of people who had been subject to an unpleasant situation fairly easily gave up when the experience was repeated. He called this 'learned helplessness'. When they couldn't overcome the situation the first time they didn't even try the second time. So what was different about the one-third who didn't give in? How did they bounce back?

The 'bouncers', he discovered, are people who regard setbacks as temporary, local and changeable. They avoid the kinds of negative thinking described earlier in the chapter. In particular they don't, in the jargon, 'catastrophize'. That is, they don't exaggerate problems. They don't say: 'My whole life has been ruined.' They don't say: 'No matter where I go it will always be the same.' They don't say: 'There's nothing I can do about this.'

'Bouncers' are optimists. They see a way out. And in fact many of them are stronger after a calamity than they had been before. You, too, can be stronger.

Try it now: Challenge yourself

If you can eradicate the ten kinds of negative thoughts described earlier you will automatically become much more resilient. But there is also something else you can do. Challenge yourself. Some people deliberately seek out situations they find difficult. They enjoy the excitement. They get an adrenaline buzz. But those challenges also build confidence and help them get problems into perspective. You, too, can build resilience in the same way.

Here's how. Write down three things that are a frequent source of anxiety for you. Next, set yourself challenges that will confront those fears head on. Don't make them too difficult. Just aim to go that little bit further than you've gone before. For example, if you're nervous about speaking in public join a debating society. If you're scared of heights go climbing or abseiling. If you find it difficult to talk to the opposite sex take dancing lessons. When trouble comes along, say to yourself: 'I survived abseiling down a cliff so I can easily handle this crisis.' Or: 'I gave a speech in front of 500 people so I can easily handle this interview.' Or: I've danced with some very attractive partners so I know I can approach that man/woman with confidence.' Make self-challenges a habit and keep on growing.

Applying the lessons to your past

We've started to work on your present and future. But what about your past? Does your past bother you? Does it make you unhappy? Then why not change it? Let's apply some of the lessons we've just learned.

But surely, you say, we can't change our past lives? Surely we can't change the facts of history? Well, no, we can't change the facts but are you sure they are the facts? We only remember a tiny fraction of past events and, to some extent, we choose our memories to fit with the world view we've selected for ourselves. Some people choose to remember the best and some choose to remember the worst.

Are you, for example, one of the many people who has been through a separation or divorce? What, then, are your memories of your ex-partner? Can you remember that you once loved him or her? Or can you only recall the rows and the flying saucepans? Do you only want to remember the rows and the flying saucepans? That's most likely the case. But there was a time when you were in love. There was a time when you were happy together. Why not remember those times?

This doesn't mean pretending that the bad things never happened. You may, indeed, have to face up to those bad things and deal with them. But it may be that you have feelings of bitterness and resentment that are spoiling your present life and yet which aren't justified. There is a different way of looking back at things. Consider these statements, for example:

▶ I should never have married, but then, inevitably, we make mistakes when we're young.

▶ We had some good years together.

▶ We had some difficult times but I learned from them.

▶ It's fortunate we split up because I'm now able to fulfil myself in a more suitable relationship.

▶ I've made my new relationship much stronger than it ever would have been if I hadn't got those past experiences to draw on.

These are all positive ways of looking at the past. You'll be much happier if you adopt the same mindset.

Remember this: Look back in happiness

Your past can be a rich source of pleasure if you allow it to be. Don't cut yourself off from it simply because a few things turned out badly. Yes, looking back can make you feel bitter. But it can also make you extremely happy. It's your choice.

Try it now: Review the day

Every day find a quiet time to mull over your past. When you go to bed can be a good moment. Re-examine those events you think of as negative and which bother you. Ask yourself these questions.

* Were they really as uniformly black as I've painted them? Wasn't there maybe a little grey, too, or even white?
* Am I applying standards that would have required perfection on the part of myself or others?
* Am I exaggerating the negative?
* Am I applying glib labels with the benefit of hindsight?
* Is it really the case that I, or others, should have behaved differently?
* Am I wrongly taking responsibility for things?

Sometimes events bother us more in retrospect than they did at the time. Also ask yourself this: 'Am I seeing the past through my eyes now or my eyes then?'

Case study: John

For a long time John felt rather bitter about his schooldays. 'I didn't like the rules,' he says. 'I thought they were very unjust and looking back made me angry. Then I realized that, intended or not, my schooldays made me into a person who has fought against injustice ever since. I realized I should be grateful. And now I am.'

Try it now: Tune it out

If you're having a problem with an unpleasant or embarrassing memory you may be able to desensitize yourself through the power of music. Here's how. Recall the scene and, at the same time, 'play' some music in your mind that is completely incongruous. In most cases you'll want it to be something humorous – perhaps the theme from your favourite comedy programme. In other words, it's as if you're watching a film with the wrong soundtrack. Do this several times. Check your response by recalling the scene again but this time without the music. Hopefully you'll find you're a lot less upset by the memory than you had been.

Why are we negative?

It's worth asking why you or anybody else should want to look at things in a negative way. After all, if looking for the positive leads to happiness and if looking for the negative leads to everything bad, then only a fool would look for the negative. And yet so many people do.

According to many psychiatrists and psychologists, infants very quickly develop into one of four types, after which it's rather difficult to change:

1 I'm all right and you're all right.

2 I'm all right but you're not all right.

3 I'm not all right but you're all right.

4 I'm not all right and you're not all right.

You can probably grasp right away that the first of these is most likely to lead to happiness. The second will lead to occasional happiness. The third and fourth are recipes for unhappiness.

> It is not the strongest of the species that survive, nor the most intelligent, but the one most responsive to change.
> Charles Darwin (1809–82), English scientist

Keep smiling

Welcome to the psychotherapy hotline:

If you are obsessive-compulsive, please press 1 repeatedly.

If you are co-dependent, please ask someone to press 2.

If you have multiple personalities, please press 3, 4, 5 and 6.

If you are schizophrenic, listen carefully and the voices will tell you which number to press.

If you are depressed, it really doesn't matter what number you select because no one will answer anyway.

Breakthrough

Now that you've read about the ten negative ways of thinking, what do you feel about them?

1 I agree that some are negative but I still see others as positive.

2 I agree they're all negative but, in practice, I just can't help thinking that way.

3 I've now stopped thinking in any of those negative ways.

I certainly wouldn't expect anybody to answer '3' at this stage, but if you did, or if you agreed that most of the ten ways of thinking were negative, you've made a breakthrough and you're ready to move on to the next chapter. If, however, you think most of the ten ways of thinking are actually positive, then you're not yet completely focused on happiness. Yes, comparing with others often acts as a spur to strive harder; yes, greed is often an ingredient in amassing enormous wealth; yes, perfectionism may lead to a great work of art – eventually. But we're concerned with happiness, not with getting rich or having a painting in a famous art gallery. Being consistently happy requires a different mindset. Spend a little time reflecting on what you really want in life. Are you going to sacrifice happiness to achieve other goals? Or are you going to make happiness your goal?

Focus points

The main points to remember from this chapter are:

* your brain is plastic, which means it can be rebuilt as a 'happy brain'
* the best way to change your brain is to change your thoughts
* cognitive therapy (CT) is a highly effective way of changing your thought patterns
* there are (at least) ten unhappy, negative ways of thinking that need to be tackled
* you can change your past as well as your present and your future.

Keep smiling

> The fact that no one understands you doesn't mean you're an artist.

Next step

You've tackled the ten negative ways of thinking. In Chapter 3, we're going to come at happiness from a slightly different direction. We'll be looking at ways of eradicating negative emotions.

3

Cultivating positive emotions

In this chapter you will learn:

- ▶ *how negative emotions can harm you*
- ▶ *the antidotes to negative emotions*
- ▶ *how laughter can beat stress.*

I like living. I have sometimes been wildly, despairingly, acutely miserable, racked with sorrow, but through it all I still know quite certainly that just to be alive is a grand thing.

Agatha Christie (1890–1976), English crime writer

In the previous chapter we looked at unhappy, negative ways of thinking and how to change them. In this chapter we're going to take a look at unhappy, negative emotions and how you can overcome them. If you don't, the person they'll harm is... you.

As usual, let's begin by finding out what stage you're at right now.

Self-assessment: How negative are my emotions?

For each of the following groups of statements choose the one that most closely reflects your outlook.

1 When I feel angry with someone:

   a I always ask for their point of view – quite often I don't then feel angry any longer

   b I try my best not to show it but kick the cat instead

   c I shout at them – it's important to clear the air.

2 When I realize I'm in the wrong:

   a I always apologize

   b I do my best to conceal it

   c I try to put the blame on someone else.

3 I believe:

   a I'm okay and that other people are okay, too

   b I'm okay but I'm always wary of other people

   c I'm not okay, which is probably why I look up to most other people

   d no one is okay – and I include myself.

4 I believe most people:

   a will try to help you once they get to know you

   b are out for what they can get.

5 If someone does something against me:

   a I try not to dwell on it – the desire for revenge just makes you bitter and unhappy

   b I'll always try to get even.

6 In confrontational situations:

   a I always try to diffuse the situation with a joke or a laugh

   b I'm usually the one to back down

   c I believe attack is the best defence.

7 When I see wealthy people in expensive cars or going into luxury hotels or shops:

   a I still prefer being me – jealousy is futile

   b I'm motivated to try all the harder in my career

   c I envy them so much it spoils my day.

8 I love my partner but:

   a there are no 'buts'

   b I suspect he/she doesn't really love me

   c I resent the way I'm treated sometimes.

9 I laugh:

   a frequently

   b maybe once or twice an hour

   c maybe once or twice a day

   d very little – some days not at all.

10 When I make a mess of something:

   a I don't give myself too hard a time – no one is perfect

   b I feel guilty.

So how did you score? For this chapter I've selected ten emotions that can damage your life. If you mostly selected 'a', you don't suffer from them very much. But if you mostly opted for other answers, this chapter could make a big difference to your happiness.

No doubt you can add some other negative emotions to the list. But I'm focusing on these ten because in our society, to a greater or lesser extent, they're often considered to be prudent, appropriate and even beneficial. You've probably lived with them all your life and never questioned them – until now.

We believe, for example, that anger fuels action. We believe that cynicism protects us from trickery. We believe we are defined by the people and things we hate just as much as by the people and things we like. But if you're going to be truly happy, you first have to unlearn those kinds of negative ideas. Not only do they poison the mind, they also damage the physical body and lead to various diseases.

Here, then, are the ten potentially damaging emotions: anger, blame, cynicism, guilt, hate, indifference, jealousy, resentment, revenge, suspicion.

And here are the antidotes: empathy, forgiveness, kindness, patience, sympathy, tolerance, understanding.

Remember this: Strange but true

You're probably going to find some of the ideas in this chapter strange at first. They're far from the normal Western way of looking at things. And they can seem to demand almost superhuman qualities. But try this new way and you may be surprised to find it easier than you imagined. And the rewards, in terms of happiness, are enormous.

Feeling good about other people

Anger builds more anger. And more anger builds hate. There's quite a lot of scientific data to prove it, but it's not really necessary to refer to that to know that it's true. We all know how we can 'goad' ourselves on. And we also know how other people respond. In Eastern thought, as well as physics, every action creates an equal and opposite reaction.

It's one of the most important lessons you can learn when dealing with yourself and with other people. Anger is the way to escalate a situation, both internally and externally. The idea that you can get rid of your anger by letting it out is a popular one but misguided. Shouting at somebody, or shouting at an empty chair which represents somebody or punching pillows, is the exact opposite of what's needed. The best way to counter anger is to understand the other person's position. In other words, let the other person explain why they said or did what they did and, if you still feel angry, explain in turn how you feel and why. That's always a good idea but it's completely different to venting your anger, as if it's steam escaping from a pressure cooker. What you actually need to do is turn off the heat.

If you are going to let your anger out, then let it out as laughter (see later in this chapter). And there's another very good reason to eliminate negative emotions; quite simply, negative emotions make you ill.

Key idea: Don't build an angry brain

From what you now know about the workings of your brain you can see the danger. When you allow your anger to build up you're actually strengthening the 'anger synapses' in your brain. You're moulding your brain for anger. Far from getting rid of the anger, you're unintentionally redesigning the capacity of your brain to create more anger. It's a disaster, as when you're angry you can't be happy.

How negative emotions are dangerous for your health

Negative emotions are assassins. And the person they're stalking is you.

A link between emotion and illness has long been postulated but it was only in the 1970s that psychologist Robert Ader uncovered one of the mechanisms. He gave rats saccharin-flavoured water along with a chemical that suppressed T-cells (key parts of the immune system). Later he gave just the saccharin-flavoured water but the rats' T-cell count still went down. The significance of the experiment was that it proved a connection between the brain (which 'tasted' the water) and the immune system.

Soon afterwards, David Felten, a colleague of Ader's at the University of Rochester's School of Medicine and Dentistry, pinpointed synapse-like contacts where the autonomic nervous system (responsible for 'running' the body) spoke to the immune cells using neurotransmitters.

There's at least one other mechanism connecting emotions and physical health. During stress, the body releases a cocktail of hormones, including adrenaline (epinephrine), noradrenaline (norepinephrine), cortisol and prolactin. Generally speaking, these 'stress hormones' have the effect of suppressing the immune system. Why evolution should have arranged things that way can only be conjectured. Possibly it's a method of conserving energy during an emergency.

The problem is that if stress is prolonged or constant (if, for example, you nurture your negative emotions), then your immune system will be permanently compromised.

What's more, stress hormones lead to higher levels of glucose, cholesterol and fat in the blood, to provide the energy for physical action. But if physical action doesn't follow (and, in our society, it usually doesn't), plaque gets deposited on the walls of the blood vessels, which can be a risk to health in the longer term. To that long-term risk is added the short-term risk of heart attack when noradrenaline levels are sharply elevated.

A list of the disorders in which negative emotions play some sort of role includes: allergies, asthma, cancer, colds and flu, depression, diabetes, headaches, heart disease, hypertension, indigestion, muscle pain and cramps, sexual problems, strokes and ulcers.

The conclusion is simple: be happy, stay healthy.

Remember this: Protect your peace of mind

Look upon your peace of mind and happiness as a great treasure that has to be protected at all costs. It's not something with which you can take risks. Think of it like one of your children. Or the greatest love of your life. When anything threatens it, take evasive action immediately.

Learning to empathize

The way to protect your peace of mind and happiness is with empathy. Don't make the mistake of thinking that empathy is primarily for the benefit of another person. Empathy is also for your benefit. Let's take a simple everyday example.

Your partner dents the car. You become angry. Why? Did your partner do it intentionally? Of course not. Have you ever dented a car? Probably. Will you dent a car at some time in the future? Certainly. Will your anger make the dent disappear? Absolutely not. So what purpose is served by your anger? What benefit does it bring you or anybody else? The truth is that it does you harm.

Ask yourself these questions:

▶ how would I have felt if I'd dented the car?

▶ how must my partner have felt?

▶ how would I like to be treated if I dented the car?

In other words, you need to empathize, that's to say imaginatively enter into another person's situation.

Remember this: Anger is dangerous

Millions of people have died because others lacked empathy. Anger built more anger, which built hate. And hate led to killing on a massive scale. You only have to look at conflicts all over the world, past and present, to understand this.

Keep smiling

> When you are angry at a neighbour walk a mile in his shoes. Then you'll be a mile away… and you'll have his shoes.

Try it now: Cultivate empathy

For the next week, do your best to empathize with everyone you're in contact with, especially anyone with whom you're in conflict. When someone is angry with you, do your best not to get angry back. Just as you can 'send' your mind to a part of your own body to see how it feels, 'send' your mind into the other person to see how they feel. Before you ask any questions out loud, try to imagine why they're behaving as they are. Don't label them as, say, troublemakers or neurotics, and don't try to reduce the situation to an issue of black and white but look for the grey (see Chapter 2 if you've forgotten about these negative thought patterns). Start from the position that the other person is a perfectly reasonable human being (normally a correct assumption) and must have a valid reason for their behaviour.

Now, in a calm tone of voice, ask questions. How do you see the situation? What would you like to do about it? What is it that's making you angry? Why are you so upset about this?

When the other person replies, don't focus on the things you disagree with. Instead, do your best to find something to agree with.

When you do this, you'll defuse the other person's anger as well as your own. Then, with both of you in a more positive frame of mind, you can start to sort out the areas of disagreement. And hopefully reach a happy conclusion.

Let's say, for example, you've been asked to do something in connection with work. You haven't done it for sound professional reasons. But, for the moment, you haven't got much chance to go into that because the other person is really angry and aggressive (too much testosterone, as we'll see in Chapter 4):

Other person: You're utterly incompetent!

You: I can understand why you feel that way.

Other person: Can't you ever do anything right?

You: I agree that I haven't done what you asked.

It isn't easy to respond like this but if you do, the other person is almost certainly going to calm down a bit. Having defused the situation you can then go on to explain:

You: I have to do what's correct and on this occasion...

The other person is behaving badly but it isn't going to help the situation if you do the same. You know the problems you've encountered but the other person doesn't. Yet!

Of course, you could have responded in kind:

You (shouting): You're the one who's incompetent! Your instructions were stupid.

But that's hardly likely to lead to happiness for anyone.

Now let's turn it around. This time it's you who's asked for something to be done and it's the other person who, apparently, has failed to do it. But your approach is going to be very different:

You: I note that you haven't yet done that job I asked you to do. Is there some problem that we need to discuss?

Other person: I'm very glad you've asked me that because, actually, there is.

Now you have the opportunity to resolve the situation together and maybe you can learn something as a result. You'll find that happiness is far more likely to come from sympathizing with the person who has 'failed' than from being critical.

- The other person will be a friend rather than an enemy.

- The other person will be more likely to treat you reasonably when you 'fail'.

- You'll have no reason to feel negative emotions, which are destructive.

You may fear that everyone will think you're weak. Not at all. On the contrary. They're going to admire your insight, wisdom and, above all, your imperturbability.

Consider this situation. Let's say you go to a pub for a quiet drink. In the bar there's a man who's drunk and aggressive. He insults you, hoping for a fight. What do you do? What's strong and what's weak? Here's a clue. If you fight him, you've let him dictate how your evening will proceed.

Remember this: Other people's failures

Some people secretly welcome other people's failures because they can then take pleasure in being superior. But that isn't the way to happiness. Instead, take pleasure in being helpful.

Blame, resentment and revenge

Ideally you need to resolve a situation when it occurs without carrying any emotional poisons with you into the future. But so often it isn't like that. Let's take a common relationship problem. One partner suggests sex and the other then announces a headache. As a result, the first partner sulks.

This is the thinking: 'This is always happening. My partner never wants to have sex with me, doesn't like sex and obviously has a problem. It's clear my partner doesn't really love me at all. I'm looking for the world's greatest love affair and this clearly isn't it. This relationship is a waste of time.'

(You'll recognize the negative styles of thinking from Chapter 2, including black-and-white, exaggeration, jumping to negative conclusions, perfectionism and labelling.)

The result is resentment and a desire for revenge. These are the kinds of thoughts:

▶ I can't be treated like that.

▶ I'll teach my partner a lesson.

▶ I'll make my partner suffer.

▶ I'll pay my partner back several times over.

These are particularly destructive emotions, especially in a relationship. If you think in these terms, you cause immense unhappiness not only for your partner but also for yourself. While you have those kinds of thoughts, you just can't be happy.

It's easy to see why. You:

▶ cut yourself off from your partner's company

▶ stop enjoying things together

▶ deny yourself physical contact

▶ prolong negative emotions for hours or even days

▶ make yourself physically ill.

In short, to use an old cliché, you 'cut off your nose to spite your face'.

The right course is to accept that your partner does have a headache. You should ask if there's anything you can do (a painkiller, a cup of tea, taking over your partner's chores). All the while, you should be thinking like this: 'My partner and I have been together for years and we've had some incredible sex. I love my partner and I know my partner loves me and wouldn't deliberately do anything to upset me. We can't expect to be perfectly synchronized for sex. That's asking the impossible.'

As a result of which, you remain happy and probably enjoy sex a few hours later.

Key idea: Be positive, not negative

Let's suppose your partner actually has gone off sex for some reason.
Then you need to discuss it in a positive way and see what the best thing
to do is. Taking a negative stance just isn't going to move things forwards.

Keep smiling

> I have never hated a man enough to give him back his
> diamonds.
>
> Zsa Zsa Gabor (b. 1917), Hungarian–American actress

Try it now: No one is perfect

Would you accept that you're especially sensitive about certain issues?
That you have the odd weakness or two? That you're inhibited in certain
areas? Then next time you have a disagreement with someone, remember
you both have vulnerabilities and weaknesses.

Rather than focusing on theirs, begin with your own. Don't list their
failings in your mind – list your own failings. Not in a self-critical way;
just remind yourself, for the purpose of balance, that you also sometimes
make mistakes and that that's perfectly normal. Your desire for revenge
will go.

Because someone doesn't behave as you want, it doesn't mean they're
deliberately out to oppose you. Some issue in their lives may be inhibiting
them. Do your best to help other people tackle the issues in their lives.

FORGIVENESS

'To err is human, to forgive divine.' It's a very wise saying
because forgiving is extremely good for your health and
happiness. And not forgiving can cause anxiety, depression,
heart problems, chronic pain and premature death. Put like
that, there's really no argument.

▶ Forgive – stop turning the situation over in your mind and let
it go.

▶ When it's you who's in the wrong, apologize without making
excuses.

A useful technique for letting go is 'dissociation'. When we're really annoyed or upset about something, then in our minds we see it 'close up'. We make it as vivid as possible and, consequently, make our emotions equally strong. In order to let go, you need to do the opposite. You need to dissociate.

Try it now: Be a film director

Think of someone you've been annoyed with. Call to mind the incident that's the cause of the problem. 'See' it right in front of you. Now pull back the 'camera' of your mind's eye, just as a camera pulls back in a film.

Keep pulling back until the incident is just a tiny speck in the distance, so far away and indistinct you can no longer make anything out. As a result, your negative emotions will be much weaker and more easily dealt with. It's a particularly useful technique for handling unhappy situations about which, in practical terms, you can do absolutely nothing.

Eliminating guilt

If you feel guilty, give yourself a pat on the back. Congratulations. You're a member of the human race and a creditable one at that. But from now on I want you to stop. Stop feeling guilty. Because guilt is a futile emotion which stands in the way of happiness.

Guilt is one of the issues about which people tackle me most often. They object to me saying that guilt is pointless. They tell me that if people didn't feel guilty when they did bad things then they would do more and more bad things. But the fact is that guilt is an emotion you feel *afterwards*. So it doesn't stop you doing bad things. All it does is make you feel unhappy about something that can't be changed *and that you already know was wrong*. That's why it's futile.

Beating yourself up over it isn't going to help anybody.

The final test is this. Does guilt make you feel happier? Obviously not. So it has to go. Will you now become some terrible person? A gangster? A murderer? Of course you won't.

You're a nice person. You care about other people. You do your best. That isn't going to change. Everyone makes mistakes. You've made some and you'll make more but you'll try not to make the same mistake twice. Right?

Try it now: Eliminate guilt

So how can you stop yourself feeling guilty? Well, one thing you can do is try to get your failings into perspective. For sure none of the things you feel guilty about compares with the following:

✳ Twelve publishers rejected J. K. Rowling's first Harry Potter book.

✳ In 1962 Decca Records turned down a group that went on to be known worldwide as The Beatles.

✳ Nelson Bunker Hunt and his brother Herbert cornered the world's silver stocks during the 1970s but when the price collapsed in 1980 they lost billions of dollars.

✳ In 1983 the German magazine Stern paid around US$3.8 m for Hitler's diaries. They turned out to be fakes.

✳ In 2003 a hunter in California lit a signal fire that spread to become the largest conflagration in the state's history, destroying more than 2,000 homes and killing 14 people.

Probably none of the things you feel guilty about were on that sort of scale. Probably they're more personal. Perhaps you feel guilty that you didn't spend enough time with your children when they were growing up, or with your parents when they were dying, or that you cheated on your partner or dented the new family car. Here's a six-point plan for overcoming guilt:

1   Check that the thing you feel guilty about truly was your responsibility (see Chapter 2 'If it's wrong, it must be my fault')

2   Reflect that life is a process of learning and that you've now learned

3   Resolve that you'll never again do the thing that has made you feel guilty

4   Apologize for doing the thing that has made you feel guilty

5   If possible, put right the thing that has made you feel guilty

6   Forgive yourself for whatever can't be put right.

Keep smiling

> A woman goes to see a therapist. 'Whenever I meet a nice guy,' she tells him, 'I always end up going to bed with him, but in the morning I feel guilty.'
>
> 'I see,' says the therapist. 'So you want me to increase your resolve in turning down sex.'
>
> 'No, no,' says the woman, aghast. 'I want you to fix it so I don't feel guilty any more.'

As the old saying goes, nobody is perfect. Buddhists believe that's why you have to keep returning to Earth so you can progress further. Buddhists say nobody can achieve perfection in one lifetime and, whether you believe in reincarnation or not, that much is certainly true.

Remember that success is a very poor teacher. Success never requires that you examine yourself. Failure, on the other hand, is a very good teacher. Never be afraid of failure – just make sure you learn from it.

Key idea: Never give up

Nobody has really failed until they give up. So don't give up. You may fail to climb a mountain today but you could be on the summit next month or next year. As long as you keep learning and keep trying, there's always a chance.

> It is not how much we have, but how much we enjoy, that makes happiness.
>
> Charles Spurgeon (1834–92), English preacher

Try it now: The negative is positive

The idea of this exercise is to understand how your failures have actually been positive experiences. On a sheet of paper, write the heading 'Failures' on the left-hand side and the heading 'Benefits' on the right-hand side. Now enter something you consider to have been a failure in the left-hand column. For example, you might put: 'Went for interview but didn't get job.' In the right-hand column list all the lessons you've learned as a result. For example, you might put: 'Was floored by several questions but have now worked out good answers.' Think of as many lessons as you can, then repeat the whole process for more 'failures'.

The stress buster

In Chapter 1, I advised you to practise smiling even when you don't have a reason to smile. I hope you've been doing it. Because now I'm going to ask you to do something even harder. I want you to laugh without having any particular reason to laugh.

Why? Because laughter is a great stress buster. It can de-stress you. It can de-stress other people. It can de-stress the whole situation. And the easier you can turn it on the better. It doesn't even have to be 'authentic' laughter. As we all know, a placebo – pretend medicine – can prove highly effective. And pretend laughter is the same. What's more, it can do something a placebo can't. It can turn itself into the real thing. Start laughing and, quite soon, you – and everyone else – may find it's the genuine article.

> We don't laugh because we're happy, we are happy because we laugh.

> William James (1842–1910), American psychologist

> Laughter doesn't need a reason to be – in fact, laughter is unreasonable, illogical and irrational. Laughter exists for its own sake.

> Annette Goodheart (1935–2011), laughter specialist

Try it now: Laugh

I'd like you to laugh right now. Don't worry if there are other people around. They'll simply assume you're reading a very funny book. In fact, if you're in a public place, maybe a train, hold this book up so everyone can see it and really give your best belly laugh. Did you do it? Then, thanks for the advertisement.

FORTY LAUGHS A DAY

When we're young, laughter comes fairly easily. It starts as early as three weeks, according to some scientists, and certainly by four months. (Unfortunately, as far as is known, no baby ever learned to laugh before it learned to cry.)

Small children laugh around 40 times a day but as we get older we laugh less. One researcher has concluded that adults in the West laugh an average of just 17 times a day. That's not actually very much. Scarcely once an hour in the waking day, in fact. I'm aiming to get you laughing at least those 40 times a day you enjoyed as a child.

It's not just for you. It's for everyone you come into contact with as well. Because what goes around, comes around. The happier you can make other people, the happier they can make you.

Try it now: Your laughter score

Every time you laugh today make a quick note of it somewhere handy. In fact, the back of your hand could be the very place. Just make a little mark with a pen. At the end of the day the number of marks will be your baseline – the figure you have to beat the next day.

GET INTO TRAINING

If you're going to smile, laugh and be happy more than ever before, you've got to get into training. If you were strengthening your biceps, you'd pick up weights even though you didn't actually want them, in other words, for no reason. It's the same with smiling and laughter. You've got to learn to smile for no reason. You've got to learn to laugh for no reason.

Then, in the same way that you can become capable of lifting heavier and heavier weights, so you can become capable of smiling and laughing in 'heavier and heavier' situations.

I learned this lesson years ago from a woman who taught children with a wide range of disabilities. She was always smiling, always laughing in the midst of difficulties and, at first, it annoyed me. How could everything seem so funny to her? How could she be so insensitive to all the problems of her pupils, let alone the rest of the world? It seemed to be a kind of madness.

One day, perhaps reading my mind, she explained it to me. Many of her pupils with quite severe disabilities were nevertheless happy. How could she not be happy with all the advantages she had? And then I saw very clearly my own disability. She had pupils who, for example, couldn't walk without callipers. In my case, I couldn't be happy, couldn't laugh, unless I, too, was provided with artificial assistance.

She wasn't mad at all. She was one of the few sane people. It's the rest of us who are mad. If we need assistance to laugh and be happy, then we too are disabled. So practise your unassisted laughing and cure your disability.

(By the way, if you don't live alone, it would be a good idea to explain this to everyone else in the household. Otherwise, sadly, you may find them sending for the men in white coats.)

Try it now: Comedy reruns

Close your eyes and think of something funny that happened recently. Replay it in your mind. If you can't think of anything from real life, replay a scene from a movie. Let yourself smile. Then let yourself chuckle. Then let yourself laugh. If you're with someone else, share the scenario with them.

LAUGHTER REALLY IS THE BEST MEDICINE

You probably don't need convincing that laughter is good for you. But I'm going to tell you anyway: laugh and you're less likely to get ill; if you are ill, you'll get better more quickly.

That's why in hospitals, clinics and social centres in more than 50 countries there are now more than 5,000 laughter clubs. Some were inspired by Dr Madan Kataria, who created World Laughter Day in 1998. According to Dr Kataria, our great-grandparents used to laugh four times more than we do. That's hard to prove, but the benefits of laughing are not. To capture those benefits, Dr Kataria invented Laughter Yoga – a combination of laughter with yoga breathing – and recommends 20 minutes of it a day.

But probably the most influential name in 'laughter therapy' today is that of Norman Cousins.

Case study: Norman Cousins

Norman Cousins was diagnosed with an extremely painful type of arthritis known as ankylosing spondylitis and was told he had only a 1 in 500 chance of recovery. Until that moment he'd been content to leave everything to the doctors. That all changed when he heard the prognosis, as he recalled in his famous book *Anatomy of an Illness*. 'I felt a compulsion to get into the act,' he wrote. 'It seemed clear to me that if I was to be that 1 in 500 I had better be something more than a passive observer.'

His active role was to prescribe himself large doses of vitamin C and regular injections of Marx Brothers films. 'I made the joyous discovery,' he wrote, 'that ten minutes of genuine belly laughter had an anaesthetic effect and would give me at least two hours of pain-free sleep.'

Norman Cousins may sound like a crackpot but he certainly wasn't. When he died in 1990 he had a distinguished career behind him as a long-time editor of the New York-based *Saturday Review*, had been a leading activist for nuclear disarmament and world peace, and had spent his retirement as a faculty member of the University of California at the Los Angeles School of Medicine, studying the relationship between attitude and health. His experience certainly raised the profile of 'laughter therapy', although it still isn't the universal treatment it should be.

Some doubt has now been cast on the accuracy of Norman Cousins' original diagnosis. But that isn't the most important point. The truly important point is that he was in severe pain and that laughter reduced or even halted it, at least for a while.

WHAT HAPPENS WHEN YOU LAUGH?

Let's first of all trace what happens in the brain when you hear a good joke.

► An electrical wave moves through the cerebral cortex (the largest part of the brain) within less than half a second of seeing or hearing something potentially funny.

► The left side of the cortex analyses the joke or situation.

► Activity increases in the frontal lobe.

► The occipital lobe processes any visual signals.

- The right hemisphere of the cortex is where you 'get' the joke.

- The most 'primitive' part of the brain – the limbic system (especially the amygdala and hippocampus) – is involved in the emotional response.

- The hypothalamus is involved in the production of loud, uncontrollable laughter.

So your brain is getting a good workout, for a start.

In turn, the laughter:

- increases the disease-fighting protein gamma-interferon

- increases T-cells and B-cells, which make disease-fighting antibodies

- increases immunoglobulins (antibodies) A, G and M, which defend the body from pathogens

- increases complement component 3, which helps antibodies pierce defective or infected cells in order to destroy them

- benefits anyone suffering from diabetes because it lowers blood sugar

- benefits the heart

- lowers blood pressure (after an initial increase)

- lowers stress hormones, including cortisol

- strengthens abdominal muscles

- relaxes the body

- reduces pain, possibly by the production of endorphins, but certainly through relaxation and distraction

- flushes water vapour from the lungs

- speeds recovery from surgery, especially for children.

One extra reason to laugh:

▶ It stops everyone thinking you're dull.

And one reason not to:

▶ Your underwear may get damp.

> A clown is like an aspirin, only he works twice as fast.
>
> Groucho Marx (1890–1977), American comedian

Key idea: Laughter is a painkiller

If you're in pain, you may be able to use laughter in a very specific way. Do something to increase the pain. Yes, increase it. If it's an arthritic joint, for example, move it. If it's an injury, press it. Then laugh. Keep on doing it. Pain. Laugh. Pain. Laugh. Pain. Laugh. After a while, you won't feel the pain so much.

Warning – laughing can sometimes be a bad thing

There are a few medical conditions that could be made worse by too much laughing. If you're asthmatic, laughing just might trigger an attack. It can also be bad for anyone with a serious heart condition, a hernia, severe piles, certain eye problems, and anyone who has just undergone abdominal surgery.

Case study: Jeremy

For his birthday Jeremy bought his brother-in-law a diving mask, snorkel and flippers and told him he was going to take him to a little cove where there was plenty to see. When they swam around the headland his brother-in-law, Derek, wasn't disappointed because Jeremy had deliberately chosen a cove he knew was popular with nudists. Derek was quite embarrassed when his head first popped up out of the water, but the two of them have had plenty of laughs about it since.

Try it now: A joke a day

Make a point of reading and watching something funny every day, of telling a joke and, like Jeremy in the case study above, of doing something amusing.

Breakthrough

Imagine that someone has said something you'd normally consider to be unfairly critical or even insulting. Will you get angry?

a Yes

b No

If you answered 'a' to this and the other two questions below, you've made a breakthrough and can move on to Chapter 4. But if you answered 'b' because you're still flying into a temper, go back and read the beginning of this chapter. Do your best to discuss your feelings as quickly as possible. Men tend to be quite bad at that, thinking it's more masculine to appear unperturbed, but then fuming inwardly. Learn to say things like, 'I'm disappointed' or 'I'm upset by what you've said' or 'I think that's unfair' or 'I need to talk about this'.

Have you forgiven anybody yet?

a Yes

b No

If you answered 'a' to this and the other two questions, you've made a breakthrough and can move on to Chapter 4. If you answered 'b', let's put that right immediately. Start with an easy one. Take someone whose perceived slight is often in your thoughts but not too serious. Now make the decision to forgive him or her. That doesn't mean you have to be great friends or even friends at all. It just means you're no longer going to keep that grievance on your 'scoreboard' and let it bother you. If you're finding it difficult, try a little harder to enter into the mind of that other person. See the situation from his or her point of view. If you're still finding it difficult, try thinking of the other person as a child – adults often do act in childish ways.

Have you had a laugh today?

a Yes

b No

If you answered 'a' to this and the other two questions, you've made a breakthrough and can move on to Chapter 4. But if you haven't actually had a laugh so far today, you'd better do something about it immediately. Watch a funny film, read a funny book or swap jokes with someone. Otherwise, just laugh anyway. Laughing exercise is as important as physical and mental exercise. Get practising.

Focus points

The main points to remember from this chapter are:

* get to those negative emotions early; don't let them fester, grow and spoil your life. Remember that negative emotions make you ill – be happy, stay healthy
* the principal antidote to negative emotions is empathy, which means 'sending' your mind into another person
* every action creates an equal and opposite reaction – so think very carefully before you act. When you give in to anger you build an 'angry brain' so if you must let your anger out, do it as laughter
* if the negative emotions concern someone else, discuss the problem as soon as possible and resolve it. Remember that it's better to be happy than to be vengeful
* always start with the attitude that other people are reasonable and must have a valid reason for their behaviour. So you'll be better off finding things to agree over, not to disagree over – being calm and reasonable isn't weakness, but strength.

Next step

In Chapter 4, we'll be looking at a very different way of influencing how happy you feel. We'll be looking at food.

Keep smiling

> Take a lesson from the weather. It pays no attention to criticism.

4

Eating happiness

In this chapter you will learn:

- ► *how the food you eat can help make you happy*
- ► *why you should avoid 'empty calories'*
- ► *which foods have the happiest effect.*

Let food be your medicine.

Hippocrates (c. 460–c. 377 BCE), Greek physician

By the proper intake of vitamins and other nutrients... the fraction of one's life during which one is happy becomes greater.

Linus Pauling (1901–94), double Nobel Prize winner

It may be difficult for people to describe happiness in words but scientists can more or less define it in terms of hormones. Hormones are the chemical messengers in the body that tell other chemicals what to do. One of the most important chemicals for happiness is serotonin. Without enough serotonin we feel anxious and even aggressive. With the optimum amount of serotonin, we feel calm and contented.

But where do these chemicals come from? Ultimately, they come from food, which provides the raw materials. In a manner of speaking, you can actually eat unhappiness. And, in the same way, you can eat happiness. A healthy diet is a happy diet.

So let's see how happy your approach to food is right now.

Self-assessment: How happy is my diet?

For each of the following statements, select the one that most closely represents your outlook.

1 I:

   a eat to live

   b live to eat.

2 My first consideration is:

   a how healthy a meal is

   b how tasty a meal is.

3 If I have a problem:

   a I do my best to deal with it

   b I eat for comfort.

4 I have a very busy life:

   a but I always make time to prepare fresh food

   b so I have no choice but to eat lots of processed foods and ready meals.

5 Every day I eat plenty of:

   a whole grains, seeds, vegetables and fruit

   b crisps, fried food, sugar and meat.

6 As regards breakfast:

   a I eat it most days

   b I grab a cup of tea or coffee and a slice of toast

   c I skip it but have a bun mid-morning.

7 My body mass index (BMI) is:

   a below 24*

   b over 24*.

8 I drink:

   a very moderately (seldom more than a glass of wine with dinner)

   b several units of alcohol most days

   c enough to get seriously drunk one or two nights a week.

9 As regards complex carbohydrates (such as dried beans, vegetables and cereals):

   a I eat plenty of them

   b I don't much like them

   c I avoid them because I'm slimming.

10 My energy level:

    a remains pretty consistent throughout the day

    b can suddenly drop, leaving me feeling quite weak.

* If you don't know how to calculate your BMI there's an explanation later in the chapter.

So how did you get on? If you scored mostly 'a', you already have a very 'happy' attitude to food. If you scored mostly 'b' and 'c', this chapter could make a big difference to your life – you'll understand why as you read on.

The new science of nutrition

The word 'vitamin' has only been in use for around a hundred years. Which just goes to show how young the science of nutrition still is. We know a lot more about nutrition than we did, but there's still a long way to go. It's an incredibly complex subject, and new discoveries often modify and even contradict what had seemed to be well-founded beliefs.

Take tryptophan, for example. Tryptophan is the precursor for serotonin. So it would seem to be a good idea to eat plenty of foods containing tryptophan. And so it is – up to a point. But get too much serotonin and, among other things, you'll find it extremely difficult to have an orgasm. Which just might make you very, very unhappy.

To complicate matters, tryptophan wouldn't have any effect if there weren't certain other nutrients present. You need to package it along with complex carbohydrates, vitamin B6, folic acid, magnesium and, quite possibly, other substances that haven't even been discovered yet. So you can see how testing tryptophan – or any substance – in isolation might lead to a completely wrong conclusion.

Yet another complication is that the body has mechanisms for keeping itself in balance. If it didn't, you'd undergo a personality change with every meal. And to prevent the brain getting damaged by poisons, there's a so-called 'blood-brain barrier', like a ring of hefty bouncers to stop anything other than 'VIP chemicals' from getting through. But, as at any nightclub, the desirable sometimes get excluded along with the undesirable.

On top of all that, the brain has different systems for happiness and unhappiness. They can work alone, together or against one another. A chemical can have one effect in one part of the brain and a quite different effect in another part of the brain. Pleasure and pain can exist at the same time. Happiness and unhappiness are not direct opposites.

It's because of this complexity that a scientist sometimes announces the nutritional secret of, say, long life or happiness, only for the research to be overturned a few years later.

But this is what we think we know now.

HORMONES, FOOD AND HAPPINESS

Hormones, including happiness hormones, come from amino acids. Some of these amino acids can be made by the body, so there doesn't seem to be much benefit in loading up on them in your diet, unless you're actually deficient. But other amino acids can't be made by the body. They have to come from food; tryptophan is one of these.

For adults, the amino acids that have to be eaten are:

▶ isoleucine

▶ leucine

▶ lysine

▶ methionine

▶ phenylalanine

▶ threonine

▶ tryptophan

▶ valine.

Although nowadays we have access to an enormous variety of foods, it's quite possible that we consume fewer essential nutrients than our ancestors. That's partly because so many nutrients have been stripped out during food processing and partly because we've switched to the wrong kinds of foods. A 7 kg (15 lb) monkey, for example, takes in around 600 mg (milligrams) of vitamin C and 4,500 mg of calcium a day.

Broadly speaking, that's something like 100 times as much vitamin C and calcium as is generally thought to be essential for human beings.

Monkeys aren't people, but a significant number of scientists, including the double-Nobel Prize winner Linus Pauling, have concluded that the generally accepted healthy vitamin intake for human adults is far too low. Pauling believed that human consumption of vitamin C should be increased at least 20 times, and possibly by as much as 300 times. He also had similar ideas for vitamins A, E and the B group.

It has to be said that the 'mega-vitamin' concept was, and remains, controversial, although there is a logic behind it. Human beings evolved on a 'Stone Age diet' of fruits, vegetables, nuts and seeds, along with a small quantity of fish and lean meat. Today, most people's diet is very different.

Here are some of the key chemicals that are connected with food.

▶ **Dopamine** is the neurotransmitter that makes us seek pleasure and enjoy life. It produces enthusiasm, exuberance and joy. It creates anticipation and motivation. Without it, we would never do anything. When we have a pleasurable experience, dopamine reinforces it and makes us want it again (so it's also associated with addiction). Dopamine is synthesized from tyrosine, an amino acid particularly found in wheatgerm and milk.

▶ **Endorphins** are the body's own natural painkiller or opioid, named from the words 'endogenous' (meaning 'within the body') and 'morphine'. Like actual morphine, endorphins can create euphoria. The body can be 'tricked' into releasing endorphins by spices hot enough to 'burn' the tongue.

- **Noradrenaline** (known as 'norepinephrine' in the USA) is synthesized from tyrosine. Although it's also associated with stress, in the right circumstances noradrenaline elevates mood.

- **Oxytocin**, among other things, promotes touching and affectionate behaviour, which tends to make people happy. It's lowered by alcohol.

- **PEA** (phenylethylamine) is the amphetamine-like substance that produces that 'walking on air' feeling, especially when we're in love. It is found in chocolate and some soft drinks (but there's doubt as to how well it can be absorbed from them) and is produced during vigorous exercise.

- **Serotonin** is a neurotransmitter that makes us feel peaceful, unaggressive, monogamous and content. But it reduces sex drive and the speed of orgasm, and too much causes sleepiness and lethargy. As mentioned above, it's synthesized from tryptophan.

- **Testosterone** is considered the 'male' sex hormone but it is also present in women at lower levels. It increases sex drive, but too much causes aggression and irritability. Meat consumption was long thought to promote high testosterone but at least one recent study has found that vegans had higher testosterone than either meat eaters or vegetarians. So the jury is out on this.

Remember this: It's personal

None of these qualities are absolutes. They can be moderated by other hormones and chemicals, and a lot depends on dose and personal response.

THE PRINCIPLES OF HAPPY EATING

Illness is a common cause of unhappiness, and poor diet is a common cause of illness. The general principle of healthy eating is this: you can only eat so much in a day, so make sure it's nutritious.

In other words, there are 'empty calories' that contain very few vitamins and minerals (sweets, crisps, 'junk food') and, on the other hand, there are calories that come packed with vitamins and minerals. So do your best to restrict those empty calories. In order to make sure you're getting enough of the nutrients for health and happiness, your diet each day should include the following (a cup is 250 ml):

▶ whole grains, such as rice, barley and wholemeal bread, as the foundation of at least one meal

▶ vegetables, including green leafy vegetables (about four cups)

▶ fruit

▶ nuts, seeds and legumes (about one cup).

You also need to pay particular attention to the kind of fat in your diet. Cut back on:

▶ trans-fatty acids – found in lamb, beef, dairy products and margarine (which means cakes and biscuits as well)

▶ saturated fats – found mostly in animal products

▶ omega-6 polyunsaturated fatty acids (PUFAs) – found in animal products and vegetable oils.

Maximize:

▶ monounsaturated fats, such as olive oil

▶ omega-3 polyunsaturated fatty acids – found in oily fish, rapeseed (canola), soy, walnut and flaxseed oils.

Remember this: The low-fat diet is proven

In 2015 a report published in the journal *Open Heart* questioned the advice to cut down on saturated fat. But statistics support it. In the UK between 1997 and 2007, for example, while fat consumption fell cardiovascular disease mortality in the under 75s also fell – by an impressive 55 per cent.

About two-thirds of the human brain by weight and about 75 per cent of the myelin sheath that surrounds nerves is made up of polyunsaturated fatty acids (PUFAs). The key difference between omega-6s and omega-3s is that:

- omega-6s cause inflammation, constrict blood vessels, encourage blood platelets to stick together, form rigid cell membranes and release free radicals, which destroy cells

- omega-3s reduce inflammation, dilate blood vessels, deter blood platelets from sticking together and form flexible cell membranes.

For optimum brain functioning, including happiness, you want flexible cell membranes, that is, omega-3s. But in the modern diet, omega-6s tend to outweigh omega-3s ten times over. Although omega-6s are essential, this ratio is bad. What you actually should aim for is more omega-3s than omega-6s.

Remember this: Use flaxseed oil

Flaxseed is the only known non-fish oil that provides more omega-3s than omega-6s. In other words, if you don't eat fish, try to use flaxseed oil as often as possible. When you can't use flaxseed oil, use olive oil, which is only 8 per cent omega-6.

LOW BLOOD SUGAR, LOW MOOD

The principles of happy eating described above also tie in with the need to maintain a consistently healthy level of blood sugar. When blood sugar falls below about 70 mg/dL (4 mmol), possible symptoms include:

- extreme hunger

- nausea

- nervousness

- cold, clammy skin or sweating

- rapid heartbeat (tachycardia)

- numbness or tingling of fingertips or lips

- trembling.

If blood sugar falls much further, symptoms can become progressively more severe and can include:

- confusion, anxiety, irritability and anger

- blurred vision, dizziness, headache

- weakness/lack of energy

- poor coordination

- difficulty walking or talking

- fatigue or lethargy.

In cases of extremely low blood sugar a person might suffer hypothermia, seizure and loss of consciousness.

Here we're particularly concerned with the words 'nervousness, confusion, anxiety, irritability and anger'. When you have low blood sugar you can't be happy. You might think that the solution to everything is to eat plenty of sugary foods. And many people instinctively do try it. It sounds obvious enough. Food tastes nice and produces a lovely satisfied feeling in the stomach. As they see it, a generous slice of chocolate cake is as good as the funniest TV programme. Better, because a cake can be shared with friends and you can all have a good laugh together.

But in reality, the opposite is the case. Too much sugary food is just as bad as too little. Why? It's all to do with the body's mechanisms for maintaining equilibrium (homeostasis).

It works like this. When you eat or drink large quantities of anything that's high on the glycaemic index (GI), your blood sugar rapidly shoots up. (GI measures the speed at which glucose enters the bloodstream after something is swallowed – glucose itself is 100, table sugar is 65, a cherry is 22). You may feel good at first but the effect is short-lived. To counter that sugar surge, beta cells in the pancreas pour out insulin which, among other things, should stabilize the blood sugar level. Quite often, however, too much insulin is produced and the blood sugar level falls too far, until the opposing mechanism (based on the hormone glucagon) brings it up again. If you routinely eat sugary foods, you'll constantly experience blood sugar highs and lows, affecting your energy levels and your mood. In each low you eat more sugary food and perpetuate the roller-coaster. What is more, the body eventually becomes fatigued and the insulin mechanism no longer works. That's when people develop diabetes.

Incidentally, fruit sugar (fructose) has the lowest glycaemic index (19) of all the natural sugars because it has to be metabolized in the liver before it can reach the bloodstream. For that reason, fructose used to be recommended as a sweetener for diabetics. However, the latest research suggests fructose imposes a strain on the liver that may contribute to non-alcoholic fatty liver disease. The latest advice is that fructose, either as a sweetener or as fruit, should only be consumed in moderation.

Key idea: Comfort eating can cause unhappiness

According to one study, depressed people are 42 per cent more likely to develop diabetes than happy people. The problem is that, when feeling low, many people seek comfort in things that are bad for them and for their blood sugar, such as overeating, alcohol and lying in bed all day. But that may not be the whole story. Some nutritionists also see a direct link between happiness and 'diabetes resistance'. So stay happy and reduce your risk.

Here are some tips for keeping your blood sugar at a healthy, stable level.

▶ Eat breakfast. A study by Dr Mark Pereira and colleagues at Harvard Medical School published in 2003 found that people who ate breakfast every day were a third less likely to become obese (compared with those who skipped the meal) and were half as likely to have blood sugar problems.

▶ Don't be overweight.

▶ Always go for wholegrains – brown rice, wholewheat pasta, etc.

▶ Eat plenty of vegetables.

▶ Be as physically active as possible.

▶ Cut out sugary snacks and drinks.

▶ Drink alcohol only in moderation and never on an empty stomach.

- ▶ Cut out processed foods. Not only are many processed foods high in sugar but they also tend to be high on the glycaemic index.

- ▶ Include fat and protein in a meal that's high in sugar and other carbohydrates (most non-sugar carbohydrates also get turned into glucose). Consuming fat or protein with carbohydrates significantly slows the digestion of the carbohydrates and therefore helps prevent a spike in blood sugar. It would seem that while carbohydrates raise both glucose and insulin, protein reduces glucose (but increases insulin) and fat controls both glucose and insulin.

Key idea: But some fat is essential

It's not necessary to avoid all fat in order to remain either slim or healthy. Some fat is essential to good health.

Key idea: Sugar damages the immune system

Here's another reason to cut down on sugar. High sugar consumption leads to an impaired immune system because the higher the blood sugar, the less well the leukocytes (which destroy bacteria in the bloodstream) can function. In one test, each leukocyte killed 14 bacteria under optimum conditions, but as sugar increased the efficiency fell, until each leukocyte succeeded in killing just one bacterium. After eating anything high in sugar, it takes about five hours before full immunity is regained.

YOUR BODY MASS INDEX

There's no direct link, so far as I'm aware, between a low body mass index (BMI; in other words, being slim) and being happy. Nor between a high BMI (in other words, being overweight) and being unhappy. However, being slim has several advantages which can translate into happiness. In our society, slim people are generally considered more attractive, which makes them feel good. They also tend to be considered more ambitious and more hard-working, so they tend to succeed more easily and earn more. Slim people find it easier to exercise (which is a proven source of happiness) and tend to be healthier (another source of happiness). And slim people tend to have more fun in bed.

Try it now: Calculating your BMI

The 'magic number' for BMI is 24. If you're above 24, you're considered overweight. If you're 18.5 to 24, you're considered to be at a healthy weight. Here's how to calculate it:

Step 1. Get hold of a calculator.

Step 2. Work out your height in metres squared (that is, your height in metres multiplied by itself).

Step 3. Divide your weight in kilograms by the number you obtained in Step 2.

Example:

Suppose you weigh 58 kilos and are 1.6 metres tall. The square of 1.6 (1.6 x 1.6) is 2.56. So your BMI is 58 divided by 2.56, which is 22.6. That's well under 24 and fine.

(If you only know your weight in pounds, you can convert it to kilograms by dividing the number of pounds by 2.2; to convert inches to metres, divide the number of inches by 39.37.)

This is not the place to go into nutrition in detail. If you are overweight, you should study a good book on the subject. I'll just point out that to lose 450 g (1 lb) in a week, you'd need to eat 3,500 calories less during the week, or 500 less each day – the equivalent of a sugary pudding, a slice of cake or a few biscuits. So you can lose weight, improve your blood sugar and make yourself happier all at the same time – that's three benefits for the price of one.

Remember this: Healthy eating is for life

Never try to lose weight too rapidly. Apart from anything else, you'll probably suffer low blood sugar a lot of the time, which will make you feel miserable. Focus instead on a healthy way of eating for life that gradually brings you to, and maintains, your ideal weight.

FOOD ALLERGIES CAN MAKE YOU DEPRESSED

Food allergies are sometimes a cause of low moods and even depression. The most frequent culprits are:

▶ citrus fruits

▶ coffee

▶ chocolate

▶ dairy products

▶ gluten (a protein found in wheat, rye, oats and barley)

▶ nuts

▶ soya

▶ tea.

Stress (a bad thing in so many other ways too) can be responsible for letting nutrients into the bloodstream before complete digestion. The nutrients can then go on to cause allergies. If you get allergies for no obvious reason, think back and see if stress could be the cause.

Try eliminating all suspect foods from your diet and then re-introducing them one at a time. (But don't do this if your allergy is severe because it could cause the reaction to be dangerously intense next time.) If you can't readily identify the allergen, enlist the help of your doctor.

Key idea: Vitamin C can help combat allergy

Antihistamines are the standard way of reducing and shortening allergic reactions but they often cause drowsiness. As an alternative, ask your doctor about vitamin C, which has mild antihistamine properties.

Case study: Peter

Every winter's day, but almost never in summer, Peter would wake up with a pain behind his eyes which often became a debilitating headache. An ophthalmologist could find nothing wrong so Peter decided it must be due to poor artificial lighting and invested in something brighter. Still he had the eye ache. He next reasoned it must be due to the colder temperature in the bedroom and turned the thermostat well up. Still he had the eye ache. He was now in despair. There seemed to be no solution. Then one day it struck him that there was one other thing that was different about winter. When he got home at about seven o'clock, tired and cold, it was his habit to drink a nice hot mug of chocolate. Chocolate is a well-known cause of migraine in susceptible people, usually hours after it's been eaten or drunk. Peter gave up the chocolate and never again suffered the pain behind the eyes.

Your A–Z guide to happy food and drink

Healthy nutrition is a whole book in itself. Here we'll just concentrate on foods and nutrients that are directly associated with happiness. As we'll see, some essential 'happy' nutrients are often lacking in the modern diet.

ALCOHOL

Alcohol is at the top of the list not because it's the best but simply because it begins with the first letter of the alphabet. It's impossible to ignore a substance that most people associate with 'having a good time' – but too much is catastrophic.

▶ How does it work?

Alcohol indirectly increases the feel-good chemical dopamine by inhibiting it from being broken down in the brain.

▶ What dose?

About one glass of wine a day with an evening meal would be about right. Regularly drinking more only diminishes the effect, creating a tolerance that requires increasing amounts of alcohol to achieve the same mood enhancement. The 'official' safe maximum is considered to be 21 units a week (and not more than 4 units in any one day) for a man, and 14 units a week (and not more than 3 units in any one day) for a woman. However, according to Carole L. Hart, who led a team of researchers at the University of Glasgow, the threshold at which negative effects outweigh positive effects is much lower, at just 11 units a week for a man.

▶ Any side effects?

Plenty. Some people keep increasing the dose to overcome their tolerance and end up addicted. Dopamine has the interesting ability to link with whatever visual image you're looking at when the chemical hits you. In other words, the very sight of alcohol can set off an addict's synapses. Addiction can lead to dementia, psychosis, liver damage, depression – the very opposite of the intended effect – and even suicide. Alcohol also reduces oxytocin, the chemical that makes you feel like cuddling.

Remember this: Drink moderately or not at all

On balance, the evidence suggests that light drinking improves cognitive function only in middle-aged and older people, not in younger people. And anything more than a glass of wine with dinner will do more harm than good. So the message is: drink very moderately or don't drink at all.

Keep smiling

> A man went to the doctor because his hands were trembling.
>
> The doctor asked him, 'Do you drink much?'
>
> 'Hardly at all,' said the patient. 'I spill most of it.'

BRAZIL NUTS

Brazilians are said to be among the happiest people in the world – maybe the nut is the secret.

▶ How does it work?

Brazil nuts contain more selenium than any other food and about 2,500 times more selenium than any other nut. Selenium deficiency causes low moods and depression.

▶ What dose?

In one study of men and women aged between 14 and 74, those given 100 mcg of selenium a day were more upbeat than controls who received a placebo. The average Briton eats under 50 mcg a day. A couple of freshly shelled nuts or half a dozen ready-shelled nuts will bring you up to your daily requirement.

▶ Any side effects?

Selenium is toxic in large amounts so don't exceed the recommended 'dose' of Brazil nuts. A fungus that can grow on the nuts is carcinogenic. Brazil nuts imported into Europe are carefully screened but, for safety, don't eat any that are yellow inside – the correct colour is pale ivory.

CAFFEINE

Caffeine is a drug that can boost mood and increase mental energy. It's very important to stress the word 'can' because it all depends on the dose and on an individual's constitution.

▶ How does it work?

It would seem that caffeine resembles the structure of a brain chemical called adenosine. Adenosine's role is to dampen down brain activity, but caffeine has the ability to displace it from the nerve cell receptor sites so the adenosine can't do its job and the brain remains more alert.

▶ What dose?

Even a very tiny dose of caffeine has an effect and it lasts for several hours. Experts say the optimum dose is around 100–200 mg in the morning and the same again in the late afternoon when energy levels often slump.

As the following table shows, the most potent source of caffeine is fresh, filtered coffee. One cup (5 fl. oz/140 mg) is all it takes. If you drink instant coffee or tea, you'll need two cups at a time to equal this dose. Despite their famed kick, energy drinks generally lag behind, at around half the strength of filter coffee (but it's easier to drink more). There's also caffeine in chocolate, but the amount in a cocoa drink is negligible. You'll get more in a bar of plain chocolate, but even so, you'd have to consume your entire day's allowance of calories to get the optimum.

Sources of caffeine	mg
Cup of filter coffee	140
Cup of percolated coffee	80
Cup of instant coffee	65
Cup of tea (bags or leaves)	60
Glass of cola or energy drink	44
Cup of instant tea	30
1 oz/30 g of plain chocolate	20
1 oz/30 g of milk chocolate	6
Cup of hot chocolate	4

▶ Any side effects?

Some studies have found that coffee can increase the risk of heart disease, and this appears to be the case even if the coffee is decaffeinated. On that basis, tea would appear to be a safer source of caffeine, especially as tea fights certain cancers and viruses and acts as an anticoagulant.

Large doses of caffeine can have the opposite of the desired effect, causing anxiety. In susceptible individuals even one or two cups can cause panic attacks. If you have these problems, it would be a good idea to cut out coffee altogether.

Which brings us to another side effect. Coffee is addictive. Fine if you can always get it when you want it. But the first day you can't, you'll be lethargic and even depressed.

CHILLI PEPPERS

Chilli peppers are a fun way of giving yourself a happiness boost.

▶ How does it work?

Chilli peppers contain capsaicin, the chemical responsible for the burning sensation. But capsaicin is also a painkiller. When inhaled it stops headaches, and when it's injected it reduces joint pain. It seems that when you eat hot chilli peppers, the burning sensation causes messages to be sent to the brain, which responds by releasing endorphins, the body's natural painkillers. With each additional pepper you get an additional rush.

▶ **What dose?**

If you're not used to hot food, start out with small doses and build up.

▶ **Any side effects?**

Chilli peppers clear the sinuses, act as a decongestant and keep the blood mobile.

CHOCOLATE

Many people instinctively reach for the chocolate when they feel down, and with good reason. But it's important to choose a variety that's at least 60 per cent cocoa, the ingredient that contains all the mood-boosting chemicals. Milk chocolate just won't do.

▶ **How does it work?**

Cocoa is a veritable cocktail of happy chemicals:

▶ caffeine (see above)

▶ theobromine is a mild stimulant that may produce arousal and a feeling of well-being

▶ phenylethylamine (PEA) – chocolate undoubtedly contains this amphetamine-like compound but its absorption from chocolate hasn't been proven

▶ anandamide-boosting chemicals – anandamide binds to specific receptors in the brain, heightening sensation and increasing pleasure

▶ 1-MeTIQ is a chemical that might inhibit Parkinson's disease

▶ antioxidants may prevent free radical damage to the brain

▶ procyanidins act as both antioxidants and anti-inflammatories; they also relax smooth muscles, which can aid erection during sex.

▶ What dose?

There is no known optimum dose but around 1 oz/30 g a day would be reasonable.

▶ Any side effects?

Dark chocolate contains around 600 calories per 3.5 oz/100 g, so you'll put on weight if you eat too much. Avoid varieties high in sugar. In susceptible individuals, chocolate can cause migraine.

COMPLEX CARBOHYDRATES

The brain is fuelled by glucose, but eating sugar isn't the best way of absorbing it. As we've seen above, eating sugar leads to highs and lows (as well as various health problems). What the brain needs most of all is a steady supply, and that comes best from complex carbohydrates, which break down slowly and release energy constantly. Complex carbohydrates include dried beans, pasta, vegetables, cereals and bread.

▶ How does it work?

Complex carbohydrates are happiness foods because they help maintain constant blood sugar and facilitate the production of serotonin.

▶ What dose?

You need about 1 oz/30 g of pure carbohydrate in order to feel more tranquil. In a day, aim to get at least half your calories from complex carbohydrates (most people don't).

▶ Any side effects?

Endurance athletes load up on complex carbohydrates to provide their muscles with the glycogen they need. But carbohydrates don't work well for everybody – some people just feel lethargic after eating rather than content.

Case study: Jack

Jack had a reputation as a very irritable old man. He was especially irritable in the morning, pretty irritable in the late afternoon just before dinner, and a touch irritable the rest of the time. A new carer suspected that his blood sugar was to blame. She banned sugary foods, introduced a substantial breakfast, increased the complex carbohydrate content of all meals, and moved dinner to a later time so Jack wouldn't have such a long gap before his next meal. Jack remains cantankerous but is never as irritable as he used to be.

FOLIC ACID (FOLATE)

Folic acid, a B vitamin, occurs naturally in green leafy vegetables and legumes but most people don't get enough.

▶ How does it work?

Folic acid deficiency causes serotonin levels to plummet.

▶ What dose?

The generally recommended level is 300–400 mcg but most people get around 200 mcg – equivalent to 5 oz/140 g of cooked spinach. Either eat more vegetables or take a supplement.

▶ Any side effects?

Folic acid can mask vitamin B12 deficiency. At very high doses folic acid can be toxic.

GARLIC

Researchers at the University of Hanover, testing the effect of garlic on high cholesterol, came up with a finding they hadn't been expecting. Garlic boosts mood and reduces anxiety, irritability and fatigue.

▶ How does it work?

Nobody knows at the moment, but garlic is packed with interesting chemicals, notably allicin, which is responsible for the smell.

▶ What dose?

One to two raw cloves a day.

▶ Any side effects?

The smell. But that goes away with regular use. Garlic also boosts the immune system, fights cancer and is an antibiotic, blood-thinner, expectorant and decongestant. Oh, yes, and it really does help men have sex – which tends to make them cheerful.

OATS

The traditional Scottish breakfast has almost magical properties.

▶ How does it work?

Oats contain tryptophan, the precursor for serotonin, as well as B vitamins, calcium, magnesium and potassium, all of which are essential for healthy nerves.

▶ What dose?

About a bowl a day would be good.

▶ Any side effects?

Half a cup of oat bran or a whole cup of dry oatmeal will lower undesirable LDL cholesterol by about 20 per cent while raising beneficial HDL cholesterol by around 15 per cent. Oats also have anti-cancer properties.

WHEATGERM

Wheatgerm is the highly nutritious part of the wheat grain that is normally removed during milling. But it will still be present in wholemeal bread and can also be bought separately.

▶ How does it work?

Wheatgerm contains tyrosine, a precursor for dopamine. Tyrosine can be made in the body, but it certainly doesn't do any harm to guarantee supplies. Wheatgerm also contains the raw ingredients for serotonin.

▶ What dose?

Realistically, it would be difficult to eat more than about
1 oz/30 g sprinkled on food or as part of wholemeal bread, but
it would be considered a useful quantity.

▶ Any side effects?

Wheatgerm can make an important contribution to your daily
requirement for magnesium, vitamin B6, folic acid and zinc.

ZINC

A deficiency of zinc is associated with poor memory, slow
response and depression.

▶ How does it work?

Zinc can rejuvenate the thymus gland (an important part of the
immune system), is an antioxidant that can work in the brain,
plays an important role in memory and boosts testosterone,
which can make you feel more dynamic.

▶ What dose?

Opinions vary, but most authorities favour 10–15 mg of zinc a
day. On that basis, most people are on the margin or deficient,
especially as less than half the zinc in food is absorbed. Only
oysters are sufficiently rich in zinc to guarantee an adequate
intake. If you don't eat oysters, take a supplement.

▶ Any side effects?

Zinc can perk up the sex life of men who are deficient.

Remember this: The 'happy diet' is the 'easy diet'

The 'happy diet' is nothing at all like a slimming diet so you shouldn't
have any problem sticking to it. Its aim is to help you to be happier. You
don't have to cut out carbohydrates, you can drink in moderation and you
can even eat chocolate. So there's really nothing to stop you. But if your
existing way of eating is very different, don't try to implement everything
at once – take it gradually.

Breakthrough

Is the 'happy diet' working?

a Yes

b I'm following it but I haven't noticed any difference

c I'm not following it.

If you answered 'a', you've made a breakthrough and can move on to Chapter 5. If you answered 'b', well, changes in diet take time to produce results. So keep on with the 'happy diet' and also move to Chapter 5. If you're not yet following it, read through this chapter again. You'll see that the 'happy diet' is very easy to implement so there's really no reason not to try it.

Focus points

The main points to remember from this chapter are:
* the food you eat can influence how happy or unhappy you feel
* sugary foods can briefly cheer you up but may later cause a miserable sugar 'low'
* don't eat 'empty calories' – that is, foods with minimal amounts of vitamins and minerals
* food allergies can cause low moods and depression
* 'happy foods' include Brazil nuts, chilli peppers, chocolate, coffee, complex carbohydrates, garlic, oats, tea and wheatgerm, and happy food supplements include folic acid (folate), selenium and zinc.

Next step

In Chapter 5, we'll see how an enjoyable exercise programme will complement and build on a healthy way of eating to produce a very marked happiness boost.

Keep smiling

Chocolate is better than a relationship because:

chocolate never snores

with chocolate there's no need to fake enjoyment

you're never too old for chocolate

you can have chocolate whenever you want.

5

Exercise for happiness

In this chapter you will learn:

- ► *how exercise will make you happier*
- ► *how to assess your happy-fitness*
- ► *how to experience the 'runner's high'*
- ► *how to design a happy-fit programme*
- ► *how to stay motivated.*

Running should be viewed as a wonder drug, analogous to penicillin, morphine and the tricyclics... Physical activity is positively associated with good mental health, especially positive mood, general well-being and less anxiety and depression.

William Morgan, Ph.D. (past president, American Psychological Association Division of Exercise and Sport Psychology)

Let's get one thing clear right at the start. Contrary to everything you may have believed, exercise makes you happy. Exercise is fun. Yes, F. U. N. There's no surer way to boost your mood both immediately and in the longer term.

Scientists can measure these things. And they've found that the levels of endorphins, phenylethylamine and noradrenaline – some of what might be called 'happy chemicals' – shoot up when you exercise.

You may remember that in Chapter 3 noradrenaline was said to be bad for you. Well, that's what makes hormones so complicated. Noradrenaline released during periods of stress is bad for you. But when you're happy – when, for example, phenylethylamine is present – you'll feel great. And if dopamine is also present you'll feel euphoric. You see, it's seldom a matter of any one individual hormone acting alone, it's the cocktail.

What's more, exercise isn't only exhilarating at the time. Regular exercise has an enduring effect that also helps keep you smiling through life's little crises.

So let's see how you feel about exercise at the moment and how 'happy-fit' you are.

Self-assessment: How 'happy-fit' am I?

The first five questions are designed to check your attitude to exercise and health – in each group choose the answer that most closely represents you. The final five questions are designed to make an assessment of your fitness.

1 Exercise makes me feel:

  a happy and exhilarated

  b bored

  c tired

  d miserable.

2 I exercise:

  a vigorously most days for at least half an hour

  b vigorously for at least 20 minutes three times a week

  c a bit at weekends

  d by doing the gardening, the chores and the shopping – that's enough exercise for anyone.

3 A person's life expectation is:

  a improved by regular exercise

  b not extended by exercise – but it might seem like it

  c all down to luck.

4 As regards smoking:

  a I never have

  b I used to but I gave up

  c I smoke a bit

  d I smoke 20 or more cigarettes (or equivalent) a day.

5 As regards alcohol:

    a I don't drink at all

    b I drink a unit three or four days a week

    c I drink a unit every day

    d I drink up to three units a day (man)/two units a day (woman)

    e I drink over three units a day (man)/ over two units a day (woman).

6 My body mass index* is:

    a 20–23

    b 24

    c 25

    d 26–27

    e over 27

    f under 20.

If you've forgotten how to calculate BMI refer back to the previous chapter.

7 My resting heart rate (my pulse when I wake up in the morning and before I get out of bed) is:

    a under 50

    b 50–60

    c 60–70

    d 70–80

    e 80–90

    f over 90.

8 After warming up and with my legs straight I can touch:

    a the floor with the palms of my hands

    b the floor with the tips of my fingers

    c my ankle bones

    d my calves.

9 In one minute I can do the following number of sit-ups:

    a more than 50

    b 40–50

    c 30–40

    d 20–30

    e 10–20.

(Don't do this if you have a back problem. To do sit-ups, lie on your back on the carpet, knees bent, heels about 45 cm (18 inches) from your buttocks, feet flat on the floor shoulder-width apart and anchored under a heavy piece of furniture. Your hands should be on the sides of your head. When reclining you only need to touch your shoulders to the floor.)

10 I can walk half a mile in:

    a under 6 minutes

    b 6–7 minutes

    c 7–8 minutes

    d 8–9 minutes

    e 9–10 minutes

    f over 10 minutes.

(Measure the distance along a flat stretch of road/pavement using your car.)

So how did you get on? If you answered 'a' in every case, you not only have a very positive attitude towards exercise and health but you're also one of the fittest people on the planet. Obviously the ideal is that you would be a non-smoker and very moderate drinker exercising vigorously for at least half an hour most days of the week.

As we saw in Chapter 4, a body mass index (BMI) of 24 is considered the cut-off between being a healthy weight and being overweight. So 20–23 would be really good. Anything under 20 risks being unhealthy, just as much as anything over 24. As regards Questions 7–10, calculate your individual scores according to the following tables and then add the four numbers together to obtain your 'happy-fit' score.

Question 7

	Men	Women
a	23	25
b	18	20
c	13	15
d	8	10
e	3	5
f	0	0

Question 8

	Men			Women		
	Under 30	30-50	Over 50	Under 30	30-50	Over 50
a	15	20	25	13	18	23
b	10	15	20	8	13	18
c	8	13	18	6	11	16
d	5	10	15	3	8	13

Question 9

	Men			Women		
	Under 30	30-50	Over 50	Under 30	30-50	Over 50
a	20	25	0	25	0	0
b	15	20	25	20	25	0
c	10	15	20	15	20	25
d	5	10	15	10	15	20
e	2	5	10	5	10	15

Question 10

	Men			Women		
	Under 30	30-50	Over 50	Under 30	30-50	Over 50
a	20	25	0	25	0	0
b	15	20	25	20	25	0
c	10	15	20	15	20	25
d	5	10	15	10	15	20
e	15	10	5	10	15	0
f	0	0	0	0	0	0

WHAT YOUR 'HAPPY-FIT' SCORE MEANS

If you scored 75–100, you are already extremely fit and no doubt already enjoying the happy bonus. If you scored 50–74, you're not in bad shape but if you do a little more you'll gain benefits in terms of health as well as happiness. If you scored under 50, then in one way you're very lucky, because you're going to improve rapidly once you start exercising regularly – you'll notice a difference in mood very quickly.

Key idea: Fitness is pleasurable

If the word 'exercise' bothers you, call it something else. For example, you could call it 'enjoying your body', or 'revelling in sensuality' or 'optimizing your physicality'. Birds swoop. Lambs gambol. Horses canter. Dolphins leap. Why? For the sheer pleasure of having a body and the thrill of moving it.

The benefits of exercise

It isn't just a matter of producing happiness chemicals. And it isn't just a matter of strengthening your heart/lung system and various muscles. It's also about improving the function of just about every part of your organism. It's about feeling vital, animated, alive. It's about feeling and being healthy.

And when you feel healthy, you tend to feel happy. In fact, in many studies, good health is rated second only to marriage as a fundamental cause of happiness, particularly for older people, who don't take health for granted the way younger people do. It works both ways: health equals happiness and happiness equals health.

But it doesn't stop there. People who exercise a little every week enjoy two extra years of life compared with couch potatoes. And people who exercise a little more – but still only moderately – enjoy almost four extra years. Those who exercise regularly and vigorously gain as much as ten years, according to some researchers.

So what are you waiting for? Enjoying your body doesn't have to be painful, boring or repetitive. Think dancing. Think skiing. Think swimming. Think volleyball with friends on the beach. Think football. Whatever you fancy.

Keep smiling

> My grandmother started walking five miles a day when she was 65. She's 76 now and we don't know where she is.

Even if you're convinced there's no form of exercise you like (you're wrong), remember this: just watching television will become more enjoyable as a result of exercising. In fact, everything you do will be enhanced because exercise not only gets the blood pumping into every corner of your body but also every nook and cranny in your brain.

In Britain, about four-fifths of people don't get enough exercise. That's an awful lot of less-than-optimum happiness. Join the one-fifth who do! You'll:

▶ feel happier

▶ sleep better

▶ have more energy

▶ look better

▶ enjoy greater self-esteem

▶ think more clearly (especially if you're older)

▶ handle stress more easily

▶ have a reduced risk of heart attack

▶ increase your levels of HDL or 'good' cholesterol

▶ lower your blood pressure

- increase your bone density
- boost your immune system
- enhance your sexual responsiveness
- increase your life expectancy.

In other words, you'll be happy-fit.

Warning

If you haven't been exercising regularly and have any of the following characteristics, you should check with your doctor before beginning an exercise programme:
* over 35 and a smoker
* over 40 and inactive
* diabetic
* at risk of heart disease
* high blood pressure
* high cholesterol
* experience chest pains while exercising
* difficulty breathing during mild exertion.

The depression buster

Exercise is so good at improving mood that it's actually become a standard treatment for depression. In the UK, the National Institute for Health and Care Excellence (NICE) recommends exercise and psychotherapy rather than antidepressants as the first line of treatment for mild depression. In fact, exercise is beneficial for all types of depression. In carefully controlled trials, exercise has performed just as well as antidepressants in combating depression, but without the side effects of drugs.

GENERATING THOSE HAPPY CHEMICALS

So why should exercise feel so good? When you think about it, it's not hard to understand how human beings evolved that way. Our ancestors had to be capable of vigorous activity if they were to eat. When their muscles screamed for respite, those whose bodies produced chemicals to ease the pain were the ones who ran down the prey and got the food. Logically, they were also the ones evolution selected. That's a simplistic way of putting it but right in essence. Nowadays we only have to be capable of lifting a can off a shelf but our bodies remain unchanged. So if we want to enjoy those same chemicals we have to exercise. Here are those happy chemicals.

▶ **endorphins**: the word means 'endogenous morphine', that's to say, morphine-like substances produced by the body. Endorphins combat pain, promote happiness and are one of the ingredients in the 'runner's high'.

▶ **phenylethylamine (PEA)**: this chemical is also found in chocolate as well as some fizzy drinks. Researchers at Rush University and the Center for Creative Development, Chicago, have demonstrated that PEA is a powerful antidepressant. Meanwhile, scientists at Nottingham Trent University in the UK have shown that PEA levels increase significantly following exercise.

▶ **noradrenaline/norepinephrine (NE)**: when generated by exercise, noradrenaline tends to make you feel happy, confident, positive and expansive.

▶ **serotonin**: the link with exercise isn't so strong for this, but serotonin is a neurotransmitter for happiness and there's reason to think exercise elevates its level in the brain.

In addition, exercise lowers the level of cortisol, a stress hormone that is linked with low mood.

There are also two further processes at work:

▶ **thermogenics**: exercise increases the body's core temperature, which in turn relaxes muscles, which in turn induces a feeling of tranquillity.

▶ **right brain/left brain**: repetitive physical activities such as jogging 'shut down' the left side of the brain (logical thought), freeing up the right brain (creative thought). It's a kind of meditation and it's why solutions to seemingly intractable problems often appear 'by magic' when exercising.

HOW MUCH EXERCISE?

Remember that we're primarily looking at exercise as a source of happiness, not physical fitness. So how much exercise does it take to boost those all-important happiness chemicals? The good news is, surprisingly little. Let's take a look:

▶ **endorphins**: the level of beta-endorphins, the chemicals the body releases to combat pain, increases five times after 12 minutes of vigorous exercise.

▶ **phenylethylamine (PEA)**: the researchers at Nottingham Trent University found that running at 70 per cent of maximum heart rate (MHR: see below) for 30 minutes increased the level of phenylacetic acid in the urine (which reflects phenylethylamine) by 77 per cent.

▶ **noradrenaline/norepinephrine (NE)**: this increases up to ten times following eight minutes of vigorous exercise.

Remember this: Ten minutes makes a difference

It would seem that around ten minutes of vigorous exercise is already highly beneficial in terms of endorphins and NE but that PEA levels are slower to augment.

HOW VIGOROUS IS VIGOROUS?

The word 'vigorous' may sound daunting, especially if you don't take any exercise at all at the moment. But, in reality, it doesn't take very long to achieve, even starting from nothing.

You've probably got a pretty good idea already of what 'vigorous' feels like, but let's pin it down a little more scientifically.

▶ **Step 1: calculate your maximum heart rate**

Your maximum heart rate (MHR) is the level at which your heart can't beat any faster. It can be worked out in a fitness laboratory but there is an easier and less exhausting (although less precise) way. To calculate your MHR, use the following formula: 220 minus your age. For example, if you're 40 years old, your MHR will be: 220 – 40 = 180.

▶ Step 2: calculate your training heart rate

Experts argue about the percentage of MHR that provides the best training heart rate (THR). But most people are agreed that, as a minimum, THR should be at least 60 per cent of MHR. Beyond 70 per cent of MHR, exercise would be classed as 'vigorous'. At 70–80 per cent you'd be in the zone where aerobic conditioning improves the most. You wouldn't want to go beyond 80 per cent unless you were training seriously to win races. So let's stick with the assumption that you're 40 years old and intending to exercise at the 70 per cent level. The calculation would look like this:

$(220 - 40) = 180 \times 70\% = 126$

At that level you should be able to carry on a conversation while exercising – with a little bit of puffing.

▶ Step 3: discover your resting heart rate

Your resting heart rate (RHR) is the level when you wake up in the morning and before you get out of bed. It's the measure of how well your exercise programme is going. The average RHR for men is 60–80 beats a minute, and for women it's 70–90 beats a minute.

If you're at 100 beats or more, you're clearly not getting sufficient exercise. You should be aiming for the low 60s or better. Athletes tend to be in the range 40–50 beats a minute. RHRs under 30 have been known.

It's not possible to say that your RHR is directly linked to happiness but there is an indirect link. If your RHR starts going down, it's a good indication that those happiness chemicals are being produced during exercise.

Remember this: You'll soon notice the difference

Don't feel despondent if you have a fairly high RHR at present. In a way you're lucky because you should be able to reduce your RHR much faster than someone who's fitter. In fact, you should see it go down by one beat a minute each week during the first ten weeks of an exercise programme (such as the one given below). In other words, you'll be able to see quick results, and that's very good for motivation.

Try it now: How to take your pulse

The easiest place to take your pulse is to one side of your Adam's apple. Just press gently with three fingers and you'll feel it. Another place is on your wrist. Turn your hand palm upwards and place four fingers of your other hand lengthwise, with your little finger at the base of your thumb. You should feel the pulse either under your forefinger or middle finger. Count for 15 seconds and multiply by four. However, it's not very easy taking your pulse accurately while you're exercising. A better idea is to buy a heart rate monitor with a watch-style display to go on your wrist. They're available quite cheaply in sports equipment shops.

Keep smiling

> The only reason I took up jogging was so I could hear heavy breathing again.

HOW LONG AND HOW OFTEN?

Asking how much exercise you need is a little bit like asking how many jokes you need or how much music you need. Come on, you've already forgotten that this is fun. However, since you ask, the minimum is 20 minutes of brisk exercise three times a week (and you'll need to allow five minutes at either end for warming up and cooling down).

Five times a week would be better. Longer sessions, within reason, would be better still. Dr James Blumenthal carried out a study on 150 depressed people, aged 50 or over, at Duke University in 1999. Not only did exercise substantially improve mood, but Dr Blumenthal concluded that for each 50-minute increment of exercise, there was an accompanying 50 per cent reduction in relapse rate. So even a little is good but more is better (within reason).

> The sooner you can take physical action when faced with stress, the less the stress will negatively affect you.
>
> Dr Paul Rosch, American specialist on stress

The runner's high

The so-called 'runner's high' is somewhat controversial. Some people say it exists and others say it doesn't. Those who say it does describe it as a state of euphoria, an altered state of consciousness or a physical style of meditation.

Of course, if the high exists it wouldn't only be runners who experience it. It should equally come with any steady, repetitive exercise. In other words, you'd be far more likely to experience it in things like running, swimming, cycling and rowing than in stop-start sports such as tennis or basketball.

One marathon runner has written that: 'Anyone expecting a high or mystical experience during a run is headed for disappointment.' But many others insist that they do regularly enjoy such a state. The explanation probably lies at least partly in the nature of the exercise – neither too little nor, on the other hand, too gruelling.

It seems that those who push themselves very hard simply experience too much tedium, discomfort and pain to enjoy themselves. On the other hand, those who don't take things far enough never get to the point at which the runner's high starts to kick in.

But it's also a question of how you define words like 'high', 'euphoria' and 'mystical'. If you're expecting to come back from exercise a changed person, a sort of instant guru, then of course that isn't going to happen.

Case study: Paul

Here I'll declare myself on the side of the 'mystics'. For a bet, at the age of 50 I agreed to run a marathon. I had just over nine months to prepare. A marathon is 26.2 miles (42.2 km) and at that point, I swear, I couldn't run more than 26 seconds without getting out of breath. I was starting from zero. Now it's a principle of amateur preparation that you never run a marathon in training. It's just too debilitating. So when you line up for your first ever marathon you don't know for sure that you can do it. In my case, the furthest I'd run was 20 miles. The extra six miles were unknown territory. Well, I did it, and for those last few miles I was flying. I'd followed a well-established training routine and it worked perfectly. I'm not exaggerating when I say I could have carried on running without any problem. Without doubt I was experiencing the runner's high and it lasted the rest of the day. (Next morning was a different story.)

Key idea: The 'runner's high' feels lovely

What does the 'runner's high' feel like? Different people describe it differently. I'd say a certain immunity from pain, both physical and mental, coupled with a sense of detachment and a quiet sort of happiness.

THE KEY TO THE RUNNER'S HIGH

I've carried on running, although I've never attempted a marathon again, and nowadays I can get a runner's high at much shorter distances. The key ingredients seem to be these.

▶ The exercise should be at around 70 per cent of MHR – high enough to generate those happy chemicals, low enough to avoid real discomfort or pain.

▶ Don't think about the exercise; instead, let your mind wander over pleasant subjects, such as your relationship or the beauty of the countryside.

▶ Stick with one type of exercise; it seems to help if the body is familiar with it.

▶ Exercise regularly – say, five days a week.

▶ Don't expect to feel euphoria early on – it'll probably take a few months before you have your first experience.

▶ You'll usually need to exercise for around 30 minutes before you start to experience an altered state of consciousness.

▶ For the first 20 minutes, while your body cranks itself up, you're more likely to be wondering why you're doing it at all.

▶ At 30 minutes you may start to feel a mild euphoria.

▶ Between 45 minutes and an hour you may enter an altered state of consciousness.

Key idea: More often, more easy

Once you've had the runner's high you'll find it comes more and more easily. You probably won't have the time or inclination to exercise for up to an hour regularly, but you could aim to have, say, a one-hour session every weekend, coupled with two to four shorter sessions during the week. During that hour-long session you should get your runner's (or swimmer's or cyclist's or whatever's) high.

Keep smiling

I don't jog. It makes the ice jump right out of my glass.

EXERCISE, HAPPINESS AND SLEEP

One simple and proven thing you can do to improve your mood is to make sure you get enough sleep. In experiments, people who were sleep deprived were more hostile and irritable, quicker to get angry, and less happy than normal. They were less likely to feel elated by good news and less empathetic to others. It's another example of 'Catch 22'. You're worried about something and sleep badly. Next day you're irritable, which means other people keep away from you. You feel less able to cope. That night you sleep even worse. And so on. It's a downwards spiral.

How can you break out of it? Exercise provides a solution. Tire out your body during the day and you'll be much less likely to lie awake at night. Don't use alcohol to help you sleep. It can *in small quantities* (take a look again at the advice in the previous chapter). But the fact is that three or more units close to bedtime are more likely to have the opposite effect, causing you to lose out on the mentally restorative slumber known as REM (rapid eye movement) sleep.

A brisk walk is much better. Also, try to adhere to a 'cut-off'. It might, for example, be 9 p.m. Up to that time you do your best to tackle your problems. You throw everything at them. But after that time you say to yourself: 'I've done everything humanly possible. I'm now going to relax and enjoy myself for a while before going to bed.'

What type of exercise?

Below are some suggestions but there are plenty of other things you can do – as long as you keep your heart beating at your THR for 20 minutes. The best exercise is something you enjoy and will be happy to do several times a week. It's no good relying on, say, a ski trip once a year or a game of tennis once a month. So when you're choosing, bear in mind practical considerations such as cost, distance from your home and the availability of friends (if it's something you can't do on your own).

> ## Remember this: Find what's right for you
>
> If you're very resistant to the whole idea of exercise, it's all the more important to find an activity that really inspires you. Something that has a point to it might do the trick. For example, rather than swim up and down in a pool, you might over the course of the summer swim along a whole stretch of coastline, getting to know all the various bays. A different kind of point can come from raising money for charity through sponsored activities.

JOGGING

Jogging is a lot of fun. The steady, rhythmical movement seems to generate more 'happy' chemicals per minute than many other activities. Just think about it for a moment. Here's an exercise that:

► doesn't require any special equipment

► doesn't have to cost anything

► doesn't require any special training

► provides plenty of fresh air and sunshine out-of-doors

► can be done indoors on a machine when the weather is bad

► can be done alone or with friends

► can be done anywhere

► enhances creative thinking and permits 'meditation'

► makes progress very easy to measure.

For all those reasons, jogging is one of the very best things you can do to get happy-fit. And even if you take up some other activity, jogging is always a good thing to build into your weekly routine.

Key idea: Take it slowly

One of the problems is running slowly enough. Yes, slowly. Beginners tend to associate the word running with 'going fast'. Wrong. Don't rush. You're aiming for a pace you can sustain over a long period. That means going a lot slower than your sprinting pace. In fact, to begin with you should try to run no quicker than the pace of a brisk walk. If you can hardly speak you're going too fast.

Here's a programme to help you build up from zero to a reasonable level of happy-fitness in just ten weeks. At the end of it, either continue at the week-ten level on three to five days or, if you really get inspired, you might like to run further.

▶ **Your ten-week jogging programme**

Exercise for 20 minutes in accordance with the following programme, plus five minutes warming up and five minutes cooling down, making a total of 30 minutes in all. Exercise at least three times a week and build up to five times. Don't run too fast – at all times you should be able to carry on a conversation.

Week Activity

1 Alternate 1 minute of running with 2 minutes of walking.

2 Alternate 2 minutes of running with 2 minutes of walking.

3 Alternate 3 minutes of running with 2 minutes of walking.

4 Alternate 5 minutes of running with 2 minutes of walking.

5 Alternate 6 minutes of running with 1.5 minutes of walking.

6 Alternate 8 minutes of running with 1.5 minutes of walking.

7 Run 10 minutes, walk 1.5 minutes, run 10 minutes.

8 Run 12 minutes, walk 1 minute, run 8 minutes.

9 Run 15 minutes, walk 1 minute, run 5 minutes.

10 Run 20 minutes.

Fun tips:

▶ Wear something crazy.

▶ Wear a heart rate monitor.

▶ If you don't want to be alone, run with friends or a dog.

Try it now: Get those trainers on

If you've got a pair of trainers and some suitable clothing, why not give jogging a try right now? Walk for two minutes, run slowly for one minute, walk for two minutes, run slowly for one minute... and so on, until 20 minutes have elapsed. Do that every other day for a week and you'll be ready to move to the next level.

GYM

If you join a gym, you'll have access to all kinds of exercise equipment. There's almost certain to be a static bicycle, treadmill, rowing machine, weight-training machines, free weights, possibly a swimming pool and almost certainly classes in things like aerobic dance and yoga.

Membership of a gym:

▶ doesn't require you to have any special equipment

▶ can be used whatever the weather

▶ can be visited alone or with friends

▶ can exercise a wide range of muscles as well as the heart/lung system

▶ gives access to a professional on hand to advise and motivate you

▶ makes progress very easy to measure.

But:

▶ you will require training before you can use the equipment safely

▶ if the gym is a long way from home you may not always feel like going

▶ gyms are expensive.

Fun tips:

▶ Buy yourself some trendy exercise gear.

▶ Join some classes.

▶ Listen to your MP3 player if the gym doesn't have music TV.

Try it now: Check out the local gym

Why not go today to a gym near you and ask to be shown around?

DANCING

Now, dancing does sound like fun to a lot of people. But can something so, well, anti-puritan actually make you healthier? It certainly can. Some people say the devil has all the best tunes but they're wrong (and we'll be seeing just how wrong in Chapter 11, which is all about happy sex). Dancing has all the benefits of jogging plus a few of its own. The only difference is that it's somewhat harder to measure progress.

Some styles of dancing incorporate meditation, such as 5Rhythms, a synthesis of indigenous dance, Eastern philosophy and modern psychology developed by Gabrielle Roth in the 1970s.

Fun tips:

▶ Wear something crazy.

▶ Invite friends round for regular sessions. Try to find your own individual dance.

Try it now: Hoof it

Put on your favourite dance music and get bopping.

DON'T FORGET FLEXIBILITY

Being happy-fit includes being flexible. So don't forget to add some stretches into your exercise routine. On your days 'off' you could also try yoga, pilates or even juggling.

Case study: Kirsten

Kirsten took her first ski holiday at the age of 26. 'It was fabulous,' she says. 'The snow made everything look so beautiful, it was sunny most of the time, and although I'd never been interested in sports I was out on the slopes all day, every day, for two weeks. I felt so full of life. When I got home it was grey and rainy and I hardly went out of doors for three weeks. I felt so low and I couldn't work out why until a friend persuaded me to go running with her. Less than an hour later I felt terrific. All my zest came straight back. Next day I was pounding the pavement again. I realize now that I have to have daily exercise, otherwise I just don't feel good.

Keeping motivated

Knowing exercise will make you happier as well as improving your health should be enough to make you throw down this book right now and head straight for the door. But, unfortunately, life isn't like that. We seldom do the things that are good for us and even if we start out with the best of intentions it's all too easy to backslide. So here are a few tips on keeping motivated.

▶ Try to take your exercise regularly at a certain time every day, and on your days 'off' just go for a leisurely stroll; then, when the time comes round, your body will soon start demanding that you do something active with it.

▶ If your favourite exercise is out of doors, try to have an indoor back-up you can turn to in bad weather.

- Exercise together with friends and jolly each other along (unless, of course, you prefer to be alone).

- Don't strain; take it easy and build up gradually.

- Keep an exercise diary and enter your distances, times, heart rates, scores or whatever; look at it from time to time and take pride in your progress.

- Give yourself rewards whenever you achieve a particular goal; if it's a cup you covet, then award yourself a cup – or it could be new clothes, a meal out, a massage or whatever you fancy (and can afford).

- Hang up a poster of your ideal body; that's how you're going to look.

- Keep thinking of the health benefits – lower resting heart rate, blood pressure and weight, fewer health problems and two to ten extra years of life.

- Maintain that 'happiness diary'. Does it show you're happier than you used to be? If you are, then for goodness sake don't stop.

Keep smiling

If God had wanted us to touch our toes He would have put them further up our bodies.

Breakthrough

So, is exercise making you feel any happier?

a Yes

b No – in fact it's making me feel depressed because it's too hard

c I'm not doing any.

If you answered 'a', you've made the breakthrough and can move on to Chapter 6. If you answered 'b' because it's been years since you took any vigorous exercise, then it's bound to be difficult at first. Certainly don't feel discouraged about it. In fact, the first few minutes of vigorous exercise are always a bit tough for everyone. It takes time for the body to 'get into gear', especially once you're over 40. And if, as a beginner, you're only exercising for a few minutes, then unfortunately it's all pain because you never get to the pleasurable part. Check with your doctor to make sure there's no reason you shouldn't exercise. If you get the go-ahead, persevere a little longer. It will help enormously if you can find an activity that really inspires you. Read again the section on keeping motivated.

If you answered 'c' and are not yet doing any exercise, read the whole chapter again. The science is there to back this up. Exercise is a powerful mood enhancer, at least as effective as antidepressants. So if you really want to be happy, don't deny yourself this proven method.

Focus points

The main points to remember from this chapter are:

* exercise makes you happy because it releases various 'happy chemicals', including endorphins, phenylethylamine and noradrenaline; it also lowers cortisol, the stress hormone
* exercise is recommended by the UK's National Institute for Health and Care Excellence (NICE) for the treatment of mild depression
* the minimum amount of exercise for happy-fitness is 20 minutes three times a week
* you should exercise at around 70 per cent of your maximum heart rate (MHR)
* an exercise diary and rewards for reaching targets are ways of keeping motivated.

Next step

In this chapter we looked at a very practical way of increasing happiness. In Chapter 6, we're going to return to the mind and discover two powerful techniques for increasing control.

Keep smiling

If you really, really can't find any form of exercise you enjoy, try the following:

start the ball rolling.

run round in circles.

jump to conclusions.

wade through the newspapers.

push your luck.

put your foot in your mouth.

hit the nail on the head.

6

Neuro-linguistic programming, visualization and self-hypnosis

In this chapter you will learn:

▶ *how your mind can be both your greatest asset and your greatest enemy*

▶ *neuro-linguistic programming for happiness*

▶ *how to hypnotize yourself.*

The stranger and enemy, we saw him in the mirror.

George Seferis (1900–71), Greek poet

Your mind is your greatest enemy. Of course, it's also your greatest asset. But everything comes at a price and the price of a mind is this. Just as it gives you the ability to remember happy times, it can equally insist on recalling sad times. Just as it gives you the power to imagine future success, it also gives you the capability to anticipate future failure. When you wake in the middle of the night you can fantasize about beautiful things, but you can also sweat over issues that, in the light of day, seem insignificant.

In Chapter 2 we looked at one successful way of getting the mind under control. That was cognitive therapy (CT) and I hope it had positive results for you. In this chapter we're going to look at some different techniques.

First, let's find out to what extent you have control of your mind and to what extent your mind has control over you.

Self-assessment: Can I control my mind?

For each of the following ten groups of statements, select the one that most closely describes you.

1 The thoughts that come into my head:

  a are generally under my control

  b are hardly under my control at all.

2 When my inner voice is being negative:

  a I just ignore it or tell it to shut up

  b I always listen to it

  c I lose confidence and can't perform properly.

3 When I wake up in the night:

  a I think about nice things and usually fall asleep again very quickly

  b I worry so much about different things I can't get back to sleep.

4 When I'm a bit anxious about something:

  a I either avoid thinking about it or I visualize a successful outcome

  b I find it difficult not to imagine a scene in which the thing I'm afraid of actually does happen.

5 When I think I won't be able to do something:

  a I visualize myself succeeding

  b I'm usually right.

6 When I visualize a scene:

  a I can see it fairly clearly and play around with it in whatever way I choose

  b I find it difficult to see it very clearly at all.

7 When I'm intimidated by a particular person:

  a I just imagine them being told off by their mother, or slipping over in a puddle, or something silly like that

  b I can't help imagining their angry face right in front of me, as if projected onto a giant screen.

8 When I face a challenging situation:

  a I always tell myself what I need to do to achieve success

  b I always run through the pitfalls I need to avoid.

9 When I have to do something that makes me nervous:

   a I first try to do something else that will put me into a really positive frame of mind

   b I just grit my teeth and soldier on

   c I usually make a mess of it

   d I try to get out of it.

10 I find that I can 'switch off' when reading a book or watching a film:

   a easily

   b only if it's really good

   c with difficulty – I keep thinking of all the things I need to do.

So how did you get on? If you answered mostly 'a', you're already good at controlling your mind through visualization and (whether you realize it or not) self-hypnosis. If you answered mostly 'b', 'c' and 'd', your skills in visualization and self-hypnosis are poorly developed. We'll be putting that right in this chapter.

Neuro-linguistic programming (NLP)

Suppose that, while reading this book, your arm suddenly began twitching? Or your head rocked from side to side? Or your legs began walking somewhere you didn't want to go? You'd be down to the doctor straightaway asking for urgent treatment. And yet, when it comes to our minds, we all accept that they can behave in exactly this same uncontrolled way. We start thinking about how to solve one problem and get sidetracked by something completely different. We listen to someone telling us something important and find ourselves wondering why they're wearing such ugly shoes. We do something that should make us happy, but instead hear a little voice whispering: 'Life is fragile – this could all end tomorrow.'

> Perception is a clash of mind and eye, the eye believing what it sees, the mind seeing what it believes.
>
> Robert Brault, writer

One day in the 1970s, when John Grinder was teaching at the University of California Santa Cruz, a fourth-year undergraduate called Richard Bandler knocked at his door and invited him to attend a Gestalt therapy group that he, Bandler, was leading. At first Grinder politely declined, saying he didn't need therapy. It was only after a few weeks that Bandler explained he actually wanted Grinder to 'figure out how to describe' what Bandler and his friend Frank Pucelik were doing as therapists. Bandler was having a lot of success and, according to Grinder, bringing about rapid and profound changes in clients, but he didn't know how to pass on his skills to others.

Grinder, who had a doctorate in transformational linguistics, was intrigued enough to attend the group and was immediately hooked. Grinder and Bandler's collaboration led not only to a detailed analysis of the methods of Fritz Perls (the father of Gestalt therapy) as employed by Bandler and Pucelik, but also later those of the 'family therapist' Virginia Satir, and of Milton H. Erickson, the leading hypnotherapist of his day. The result was a 'new' kind of psychotherapy which they called Neuro-linguistic programming (NLP).

DISCREDITING AN INNER VOICE

The first NLP technique you're going to learn is how to discredit that upsetting 'inner voice'. You know the kind of thing. Your inner voice says something like: 'How can you be happy when so many are starving?' And then, perhaps, 'you' reply: 'You're right, I can't be.' And so you're not happy any more.

Well, for a start, you could just tell the voice to 'shut up'. That's already quite good. But here's something even better. It's a technique you probably used with real people when you were a kid.

Try it now: Mock that inner voice

The idea is to discredit the negative inner voice. You may not always be able to change the message (as with CT) but you can stop paying attention to it.

The way to do that is to rob the inner voice of authority by making it sound comical, ridiculous or even contemptible. Remember how, as a child, you used to repeat something annoying someone had said, but in an exaggerated or comical tone? You can do the same with an inner voice. If your inner voice says, 'You should be ashamed of yourself', repeat the same words but as if they were being spoken by, say, Donald Duck. Suddenly they don't sound so authoritative any more.

Remember this: Your inner voice can be wrong
Just because it's your inner voice, that doesn't mean it's right.

BE POSITIVELY HAPPY

There's a big difference between stating an intention in a positive way and the same, or very similar, intention in a negative way. For example, you can tell yourself, 'I'm going to be happier in future'. Or you can tell yourself, 'I'm not going to be so miserable in future'. The two statements mean more or less the same thing. But the impact of them is very different.

In many Western cultures it's not considered 'cool' to be too eager or to show too much enthusiasm. When a friend asks how we are, we tend to answer, 'Not bad' or 'Can't complain'. It's rare for someone to proclaim, 'I feel great' or 'Life is fantastic'. It may seem unimportant but, in fact, it's a way of talking and thinking that has a profound impact on how we feel and act.

If you say, 'Not bad', you make yourself feel 'Not bad'. But that's not good enough. You want to feel terrific. So say that you feel terrific.

This business of positive and negative 'framing' (as it's called in NLP) can be extremely significant. When you use a negative sentence construction ('I won't be nervous'), you focus on the negative. But when you use a positive sentence construction ('I will be confident'), you focus on the positive. In practical terms, this can have an important effect, as the next case study shows.

Case study: Petra

Petra enjoyed skiing but she was always getting hurt while her companions seldom seemed to have problems. If they went up a steep drag lift, it was always Petra who fell off. If they cruised through trees, it was always Petra who hit one. If they skied along a narrow path, it was always Petra who went over the edge. Every hazard seemed to be like a magnet. At first she put it down to poor technique and took more lessons. But she didn't improve until a new instructor began to examine her 'mental game'. Upon questioning, he discovered that Petra was always telling herself, 'Don't fall off the lift' or 'Don't hit the trees' or 'Don't go over the edge'. In other words, everything was expressed as a negative. Instead, he taught her to frame the same intentions in a completely different positive way. 'Keep relaxed on the drag lift' or 'Head for that space between the trees' or 'Aim for the middle of the path'. As soon as she did that the improvement was dramatic.

When you give yourself (or anybody else) an instruction, the mind focuses on the object of that instruction. When Petra told herself not to hit the tree, she was focused on the tree and, consequently, her body steered her into the tree. Once she switched her focus to the space between the trees, so her body steered her into the space. Exactly the same principle applies to happiness.

Try it now: Give positive answers

Look at the following questions and responses. Your task is to change those responses from negative statements to positive statements.

- How are you? Not so bad.
- How did you get on in the exam? Could have done worse.
- Can you handle this task? I'll try not to let you down.
- How's your grandfather? He's not dead yet.
- Are you ready to give the speech? I'll try not to make a fool of myself.
- How do you feel about the news? I'm not miserable.

Having completed the exercise, use positive constructions as much as possible from now on.

Visualization

Human beings have long had the ability to visualize places they've never been to and things they've never seen. We do it all the time. If I ask you to imagine being on top of Mount Everest, you could probably convince me that you'd been there. But it's not just what you visualize that's important, it's also the way you visualize. If I ask you to visualize being very happy, for example, do you see yourself in close-up or a long way away? Is your mental picture in colour or black and white? Is there music playing or is it a silent movie? In NLP, these kinds of qualities are known as 'submodalities' and you can learn to manipulate them to create the kind of mood you crave.

MANIPULATING SUBMODALITIES

When we're afraid of things we tend to visualize them big. If you're afraid of dogs, for example, then when you think about them you probably have a dog's face completely filling your 'screen', its huge fangs bared and seeming to be the size of ice picks. When you think of somewhere you don't want to go, say a hospital, you probably have an image that's dreary and colourless. Perhaps the weight of the building bears down on you and you can even smell it. And what about when you think of something nice? Possibly the colours are warm and vivid.

The concept behind this branch of NLP is to turn everything back to front. Instead of the way you feel creating the submodalities, you deliberately create the submodalities that will make you feel the way you would prefer to be. In other words, instead of seeing the dog full-screen, you reduce the size. Instead of the hospital being drab, you paint it in vibrant colours.

Most people have probably never given a thought to the submodalities of their internal cinema. If that includes you, here's a little exercise.

Try it now: Identify 'submodalities'

Lie down somewhere comfortable and have a notebook and pen handy.

Call up an image of a person who makes you feel really happy – it could be someone close or it could be, say, a comedian. Write down the submodalities in your notebook. For example, is the image in colour or in black and white? Is it vivid or faint? Is it large or small? Is it central or to one side? Can you hear music?

Next think of someone who makes you unhappy and once again write down the submodalities.

Here are some possibilities that may help you.

Visual submodalities	Audio submodalities	Kinaesthetic submodalities
colour or black and white	loud or soft	heavy or light
large or small	high pitched or low pitched	rough or smooth
near or far	clear or muffled	hot or cold
bright or dull	near or far	constant or intermittent
moving or still	pleasant or unpleasant	strong or weak
clear or blurred		moving or still
		intense or faint
		sharp or dull
		increasing or decreasing pulse
		faster or slower breathing rate

Key idea: It gets easier with practice

Don't worry if, at first, you can't see an image very clearly or for very long. That's how it is for most people. But in order to be successful, it's essential the visualization techniques in NLP are carried out with sufficient intensity. They have to be created with feeling if they're going to release feeling to you later on. The more you practise, the more effective you'll be, so make time to carry out these experiments in submodalities every day. If you have to commute by train regularly, this is a good way of creatively passing the journey.

Once you've got the hang of identifying submodalities the next step is to begin manipulating them deliberately. Call up one of your favourite daydreams but this time, instead of just watching it, start manipulating it in various ways.

Here are some ideas.

▶ See the scene through your own eyes.

▶ Now switch 'cameras' to see the scene from another person's viewpoint.

▶ Pull back to see everyone in the scene simultaneously.

▶ Make a split screen and show different images side by side.

▶ Run a section in slow motion.

▶ Show a series of stills.

▶ Change 'camera angles'.

▶ Play some music.

▶ Play some completely different music.

▶ Use soft focus.

▶ Introduce a voiceover.

▶ Zoom in for a close-up.

▶ Move in closer still.

▶ Pull right back so you can now see for miles.

▶ Turn down the lights.

▶ Switch from colour to black and white.

▶ Have a pianist, as in the silent movie era.

▶ Have the image fill the entire 'screen'.

▶ Shrink the image to half the screen, then to a quarter, then to an eighth.

Each time you manipulate the image, ask yourself what effect it has on you. How does it affect your emotions? In particular, which are the submodalities that make you feel happier?

Once you've identified them, you can use them to make your visualizations more enjoyable, more positive and more joyful. Here's how. It's a technique I call 'the happiness generator'.

Step 1. You are the director of a movie in which you are also the star. As the director, give instructions to yourself about the way you should manifest extreme happiness. You might tell yourself, for example, to smile and laugh, to make your eyes sparkle, to hold yourself upright and dance along at every opportunity. Watch yourself exhibit the new behaviour. In your role as director, make any corrections or changes you think necessary.

Step 2. Once you're satisfied, step into the movie and experience what it's like to have this new way of behaving, as seen through your own eyes as the star. Not only see but, of course, hear everything and feel what it's like. Note the reaction of other people. Is it what you want it to be?

Step 3. If you're not happy with anything, return to your role as director, make the necessary changes and repeat Step 2.

Step 4. Now imagine a real-life situation in which you would like to feel happy but seldom or never do. Let's say, for example, that going to work makes you miserable. Look for a cue that could be used to trigger the behaviour automatically. For example, it might be the nameplate beside the door. Imagine yourself seeing or hearing the cue and immediately adopting the new, happy behaviour. Play this 'film' as often as necessary until the new behaviour feels natural.

Step 5. Use the new happy behaviour in a real situation.

Key idea: The counterfeit can become real

You may decide that acting as if you're happy is not the same thing as being happy. But in fact, as we saw in Chapter 3, smiling and laughing for no reason can indeed make you feel happy. What's more, other people will respond more positively to you and that, in itself, will also lift your spirits.

MAKING A REAL FILM

Not everybody can visualize well enough to make the happiness generator work as well as they'd like. If you find you're having problems, you could take on the roles of director and actor for real. Like this.

Try it now: Star in your own film

Step 1. Get hold of a DVD version of a film in which you've seen the type of behaviour you'd like to copy. Find a segment in which your character exhibits the behaviour and watch it several times.

Step 2. Get hold of a video camera of some sort. If you're completely uninhibited, you can ask someone to film you. Otherwise, set it up on a tripod – it will be a great help if you have the ability to connect it to your TV, which will then become a monitor. If you can't set up a monitor, you'll have to get by as best you can. (Without a monitor, you may find that on your first attempt you've cut half of your head off or something like that. Never mind. Just make the necessary adjustments and try again.)

Step 3. Rehearse the behaviour, then set the camera rolling.

Step 4. Watch the 'rushes'.

Step 5. Keep filming and watching, and filming and watching, until you think you've got the result you want. If necessary, inspire yourself by watching the original film again.

Step 6. Try out the new behaviour for real.

When you use visualization in this way you are, in effect, hypnotizing yourself. Next we're going to look at a far more direct and powerful way of achieving the same state.

Keep smiling

If ignorance is bliss, why aren't more people happy?

Self-hypnosis

The great hypnotherapist Milton H. Erickson (1901–80) sometimes taught clients how to put themselves into a trance so that they could continue certain aspects of treatment at home. The method I'm about to describe now is, however, attributed not to Erickson but to his wife Betty, who was herself a hypnotist.

What is hypnosis? Derren Brown, the TV mentalist, says he doesn't know himself what hypnotism really is. What we can say for sure is that it's an altered state of consciousness or, more specifically, a state of consciousness that's different to what we consider to be our normal waking state. In other words, a trance.

In fact, we all go into trances every day. When you're totally absorbed in a book or a newspaper and unaware of the things going on around you, you're in a trance. When you swing a golf club or throw a dart and get almost exactly the result you want, you're in a trance. When you're making love with your partner, you're in a trance.

Key idea: Stage hypnotism isn't real

Don't expect to be able to float above the ground as rigid as a board. That sort of thing is stage magic. But once you've learned to put yourself into a trance using this technique, you will be able to bring about significant changes in your mind.

Try it now: Hypnotize yourself

Step 1. Get yourself comfortable in a place where you won't be disturbed. It's not a good idea to lie on the bed because you might fall asleep. But you could sit up on the bed supported by pillows, or arrange yourself in a comfy chair.

Step 2. Decide the length of time you wish to spend in self-hypnosis. Initially I'd suggest 10 minutes. That should give you enough time to achieve a deep state of trance without feeling anxiety about 'wasting' time or needing to get on with something else. As you get used to self-hypnosis, you can vary the length of time. So, having got comfortable, you should say something like this: 'I am now going to hypnotize myself for 10 minutes.' You might like to append the actual time by adding '... which means I will come out of self-hypnosis at [a time of your choosing]'.

Step 3. This is a key step because it's when you state the purpose of your hypnosis. Here we're concerned with being happier, but you could also use the technique to make you feel, say, more confident or more relaxed or more expansive. The exact words aren't important. Something along these lines will do fine: 'I am entering into a state of self-hypnosis so that I can hand over to my unconscious mind the task of making me feel happier.' Or 'I am entering into a trance for the purpose of allowing my unconscious mind to make the adjustments that will help me feel more joyful'. Whatever you say, make sure it includes the message that you are inviting your unconscious to deal with the matter.

Step 4. State how you want to feel when you come out of your trance. For example, you might say, '... and as I come out of my trance I will feel full of happiness and ready to bring joy to my friends'. Or if you're practising self-hypnosis last thing at night you might say, '... and as I come out of my trance I will feel ready to enjoy a blissful night's sleep'.

Step 5. This is the actual process of self-hypnosis. Basically you're going to engage in turn your three main representational systems (sight, hearing, touch) to bring the trance about. In the first part of the process you will be noting things you can actually see, hear and feel *in the room where you are*. In the second part you will be noting things you can see, hear and feel *in an imaginary scene*.

In this process, some people talk to themselves internally but I recommend that you say everything out loud. For that reason you'll want to be in a private place. You might imagine that you'd 'wake' yourself up but in fact the sound of your own voice, done the right way, will intensify the effect. (If, however, speaking out loud doesn't work for you, by all means speak internally.)

a   From your comfortable position, look at some small thing in the room in front of you and say out loud what you are looking at. Choose things you can see without moving your head. For example, 'I am looking at the door handle'. Then, without rushing, focus on another small item. For example, 'I am now looking at a glass of water on the table'. Then move on to a third item. For example, 'I am looking at the light switch'. When you have your three visual references, move on to (b).

b Switch attention to sounds and, in the same way, note one after another until you have three, each time saying out loud what you're hearing. Then move on to (c).

c Note things that you can feel with your body. For example, you might say, 'I can feel the seat pressing against my buttocks'. When you have your three, move on to (d).

d Now repeat steps (a) to (c) but with only two items for each sense, that is, two images, two sounds and two feelings. They must be different from the ones you used before. Speak a little more slowly.

e Now repeat steps (a) to (c) but with only one item per sense, that is, one image, one sound and one feeling. Again, they must be different from any that have gone before. Speak even more slowly.

f Close your eyes, if they're not already closed, and think of a happy scene. To keep things simple, make it a still picture. It might, for example, be you with a group of friends playing with a ball on the beach on a sunny day. It might be you and your partner throwing sticks for your dog. It might be a scene that you would like to have come true, such as your boyfriend getting down on one knee to propose.

g Using this imagined scene, go through the same process you already used for the real scene, but beginning with just one example of each of the three senses, that is, one image, one sound and one feeling. When you've done that, increase to two examples and then three. (Three is usually enough, but if you've stipulated a lengthy session you may need to continue with your fantasy scene by going on to name four images, sounds and feelings, or five or more.) Remember, each example must be different. You'll probably find you're automatically speaking very slowly now, but if not, make a point of slowing your voice down more and more.

h After the allotted time, you should begin to come out of the trance automatically. But it may help to announce, 'I'll count to three and when I reach three I'll be (whatever you said in Step 4)'. Don't worry about getting 'stuck' in a trance. That won't happen. You may feel a little woozy for a while. If so, don't drive a car or do anything demanding until you're sure you're okay to do so.

Case study: Carol

Carol believed she didn't project happiness to other people and that she was a rather dull companion. And she was right; people tended to steer clear of her. When she got a rare invitation to a party, she determined to be different. Beginning self-hypnosis, she stated that the purpose was to 'hand over to my unconscious mind the task of making me more expansive, entertaining and warm towards other people'. In the second part of the process she imagined seeing herself at the party, standing happily in the middle of a circle of people, all laughing at the things she had to say. She repeated the self-hypnosis three times and then once more before setting off to the party. Everyone noticed the difference in her. She had a great time – and so did they.

Remember this: Keep doing it

Real self-hypnosis (or hypnosis) has nothing to do with the kinds of illusions created by magicians. One session of self-hypnosis should have a measurable effect but you'll have to repeat the process several times to bring about permanent change.

Breakthrough

You've made a breakthrough if:

▶ you've discredited a negative inner voice

▶ you are now mostly framing things in a positive way

▶ you can manipulate visualizations to make them happier

▶ you've succeeded in hypnotizing yourself.

But the most important breakthrough is simply the realization that control of the mind is one of the keys to happiness. If you've experienced that insight as a kind of revelation, then you're well on the way to becoming a much happier person.

Focus points

The main points to remember from this chapter are:

* ✳ your mind is your greatest asset but it can also be your enemy
* ✳ you can discredit a negative inner voice by making it sound comical or stupid
* ✳ always frame things in a positive way
* ✳ by manipulating the submodalities of your visualizations you can make them happier
* ✳ self-hypnosis is a tool anyone can use to increase happiness.

Keep smiling

> I used to think that the brain was the most wonderful organ in my body. Then I realized who was telling me this.
>
> Emo Philips (b. 1956), comedian

Next step

In this chapter we've seen, once again, how control of the mind is one of the keys to happiness. You've learned how to use visualization and other NLP techniques, as well as self-hypnosis, to increase that control. In Chapter 7, we're going to look at a technique that's been used successfully for thousands of years – meditation.

7

Meditating for happiness

In this chapter you will learn:

- ► *how you can experience happiness through meditation*
- ► *what meditation feels like and how to do it*
- ► *how meditation can help you be happier in your everyday life.*

In shallow souls, even the fish of small things can cause a commotion. In oceanic minds, the largest fish makes hardly a ripple.

Hindu proverb

There's a profound state of inner happiness that's available to all of us. But, unlike 'ordinary' happiness, it's not something we can create at any given moment. Rather, think of it more like a reservoir we can access. We only have to know how to get at it.

Meditation is one of the ways of accessing this inner happiness. Don't go thinking that meditation is some kind of Eastern, quasi-religious mumbo jumbo that has no relevance to your everyday life in the West. In one way or another we all meditate at times. In this chapter we're going to take things a little further and learn how to meditate more profoundly. We're going to learn how to drink from the reservoir.

Let's see what stage you're at right now.

Self-assessment: What's my inner happiness?

For each of the following groups of statements, pick the one that most applies to you.

1 I would describe myself as:

   a calm and tranquil

   b calm as long as everything is going okay

   c always on edge

   d angry.

2 Little problems:

   a don't bother me at all

   b can seem just as important as big ones

   c can make me erupt in fury.

3 My blood pressure is:

    a normal for my age

    b a bit high for my age

    c very high – I'm on medication to control it.

4 I find it:

    a easy to relax

    b only possible to relax when everything has been done

    c almost impossible to relax.

5 I sleep:

    a soundly and awake ready for the day

    b fitfully and awake feeling tired

    c very badly – I suffer from insomnia.

6 Contentment is:

    a the state I wish to live in

    b a bad thing because it stifles innovation and progress

    c boring.

7 Essentially, the world is:

    a a beautiful, wonderful place

    b fine as long as you're rich

    c a savage and miserable place.

8 On the whole, other people are:

    a nice

    b only out for themselves

    c dangerous.

9 Meditation is:

   a something I'd like to learn/have done

   b not for me

   c a load of mumbo jumbo.

10 I would/do:

   a willingly set aside 30 minutes every other day for meditation

   b never have the patience or time to just sit around and meditate.

If you answered mostly 'a', you've already achieved some of the goals of meditation. Maybe you already meditate. Certainly you're open to it. If you answered mostly 'b' or 'c', you'll find that meditation can help you a lot. So let's start meditating. Or, to put it another way, don't just do something – sit there!

You might access your inner happiness in your very first session but it takes most people a few weeks. Thereafter, meditation deepens until, perhaps after a year or two, something very profound is experienced. Almost everyone talks of feeling calmer and more peaceful. Accompanying these feelings are those of patience and compassion. Later come feelings of intense joy. And all this, in turn, leads to a more positive engagement with life.

Case study: Raymond

Raymond took up yoga about seven years ago and began meditating three years ago. For the first two years, he says, he meditated purely for the discipline. It was only in the third year that he began to experience 'strange' things. When you meet him he has a look in his eyes which suggests some special knowledge.

'I now look forward to this part of the day,' he says. 'I sometimes can hardly wait for it. It's the time when I'm alone with myself and completely in the present. I feel a connection with everything. It makes me very happy.'

So what is meditation?

Meditation is, firstly, a way of trying to get control of your mind. When unpleasant and worrying thoughts pop up in your head uninvited you'll be able to get rid of them. And when you want to summon up positive emotions and happy thoughts – when you want to draw on the reservoir – you'll have the ability.

More technically, meditation means entering a state of consciousness that is neither the normal, everyday state of being awake nor the state of being asleep. There are four categories of brain waves:

▶ beta (13–40 Hz) – the fastest frequencies, associated with normal waking consciousness and being alert

▶ alpha (7–13 Hz) – the next fastest frequencies, associated with feeling relaxed, daydreaming, reverie and light meditation

▶ theta (4–7 Hz) – slower frequencies, associated with dreaming sleep and deep meditation

▶ delta (under 4 Hz) – the slowest frequencies, associated with deep sleep.

What's the point? After all, we all sleep several hours a night in the theta and delta states, so what difference does another 20 minutes or so of meditation make? In fact, the sleeping state is quite different to the meditative state.

Key idea: The awakened mind

Notice the use of the word 'associated' in the description of brain waves above. It's possible for two, or even three or four, frequencies to be present at the same time. Although 'light' meditation is normally said to be in alpha mode and 'deep' meditation in theta mode, in practice deep meditation can involve not just alpha but also beta and theta and, in rare cases, all four. That is normally the preserve of a 'master', possessing what some call 'the awakened mind'. But everyone who meditates will combine frequencies in a way that is different to sleeping.

So the point of meditation is: to experience inner happiness. And it could also be:

► to refresh and revitalize yourself after your day's work

► to forget, for a while, your cares about the past and your worries for the future

► to try to understand the nature of the mind

► to increase your control over your mind

► to cultivate a calmer mind and a more tranquil outlook

► to develop a more balanced mental state in respect of a particular issue

► to gain a greater understanding of your true nature

► to become more totally aware.

Remember this: Meditation is good for your health

Meditation isn't only good for the mind. It can lower blood pressure and improve both the cardiovascular and immune functions as well.

Case study: Joyce

After an earlier edition of this book was published, I had a communication from a woman called Joyce who said that she rated it at just one out of ten and that most of what I'd written was too trivial to tackle problems such as hers. I suggested to her that she may have read the book but that she hadn't actually done any of the practical exercises. About three months later I heard from her again. It was true, she conceded, that she hadn't actually followed any of the advice but she'd now taken up meditation and, to her amazement, she'd quickly found herself becoming happier and more serene. Every morning she spent half an hour 'just being' and every evening she spent another half hour reviewing and tackling issues that had come up during the day.

Keep smiling

> Q: How many contemplative monks does it take to change a light bulb?
>
> A: Three. One to change the light bulb. One to not change the light bulb. One to neither change nor not change the light bulb.

Keep smiling

> Sign outside a yoga school: Yoga teacher needed – enquire within.

How to meditate

TIME OF DAY

You can meditate at any time. Some teachers recommend first thing in the morning, especially before dawn, as a way of setting you up for the day. Others recommend the late evening, when everything has been done, as a way of unwinding from the day. Still others like to take advantage of the natural tendency to feel sleepy around the end of the working day. But be careful. Sleeping and meditation are different things; although it's easier to get into a meditative state when your body and mind have slowed down of their own accord, there's always the danger of snoozing rather than meditating.

Remember this: Be regular

Find out what works best for you and then try to stick to it. Your body and mind will adapt accordingly and you'll find it increasingly easy to get into a meditative state at the same time every day.

WHERE TO MEDITATE

You can meditate anywhere. But most people like to have a special place and some also like to have particular 'props' to help them get into the meditative state.

If you're a beginner, it's probably best to have a quiet place where you won't be disturbed. Except for open-eyed styles of meditation, it will help if the room is dim or even dark. You could wear an eye mask. Make this space a nice place so that you look forward to going to it and come to associate it with meditation.

Keep smiling

> Mohandas Gandhi was asked what he thought of Western civilization. He replied: 'I think it would be a good idea.'

THE POSITION

The pose traditionally associated with meditation is the lotus position. That's to say, sitting on the floor with the right foot on the left thigh and the left foot on the right thigh, so that the left ankle crosses over the right ankle. The idea behind adopting the lotus position is that the pose is extremely stable so that, in deep meditation, you won't topple over; at the same time, it's not a position in which it's easy to fall asleep.

But the lotus position is not essential, which is just as well because very few people can manage it at all, let alone for a whole session of meditation. When you meditate you need to be comfortable. That's vital. You don't want to be distracted by thinking how painful your ankles or knees are.

If you can easily do the half-lotus (only one foot resting on the opposite thigh, the other foot going under the opposite thigh) that is good. If not, just sit cross-legged. In whichever of these poses you sit, it's important you keep your spine straight.

Rest your hands on your knees. One way is with the palms up and the thumb and forefinger of each hand touching to form an 'O'. But there are other ways as we'll see below.

Tips

* Warm up by sitting on the floor with the soles of your feet together and close to your groin. Clasp your feet with your hands and move your knees up and down like a bird's wings.
* Place a cushion under the rear of your buttocks to tip you forwards slightly and thus bring your knees down to the floor.

There are two alternatives to sitting on the floor. The lotus-type position comes down to us from an era when furniture hadn't been invented and you can meditate perfectly well sitting on a dining chair or even an office swivel chair. The key element is to sit away from the back of the chair, keeping a straight spine. Just place your hands, palms down, lightly on your knees.

The other alternative is to lie down. Many teachers frown on this as not being 'proper' and because of the danger of falling asleep. But it's an excellent position for meditating because it automatically reduces beta waves. As with the other positions, the spine should be straight, so lie on your back with your arms by your sides, palms up, and your feet shoulder width apart. To reduce the risk of falling asleep, try lying on the floor rather than the bed so you don't get too comfortable.

Key idea: Whatever works best

Don't worry too much about the pose. The important thing is the meditation, not the position. Whatever works for you is fine.

HOW LONG SHOULD I MEDITATE FOR?

You could meditate all day. But, in the context of a busy modern life, 20–30 minutes is the length of time to aim for. The longer you can devote to it, the more likely you are to reach a deep state. Nevertheless, even a minute's meditation is better than nothing. And sometimes it's possible to experience a meditative state while doing other things, such as walking or running.

However long the session, the benefits ripple out far beyond it. It's just the same as when something happens to make you angry. The incident might last no more than a few seconds but it could be hours before you feel calm again. So it is with the positive effects of meditation.

Key idea: Try a timer

Some people like to set a timer. This can work well because it removes any anxiety about not meditating for long enough or, on the other hand, taking too long and being late for the next thing you have to do. But others prefer to let whatever happens happen.

Meditating for happiness

So you're sitting or lying down. Then what? Different people use different techniques, so you need to experiment to find out what works best for you. Some people, for example, stare at a candle flame or an image or a wall; some repeat mantras; others repeat small, almost imperceptible gestures.

Here's a simple way of meditating for happiness.

Try it now: Meditation the easy way

1 Sitting or lying down with your eyes closed, notice your breathing.
2 Without forcing anything, gradually slow down your breathing.
3 Make your exhalations longer than your inhalations.
4 Empty your mind of any thoughts of past or future.
5 Just concentrate on experiencing the present moment, which is your breath.
6 If any thoughts push their way into your mind, let them drift past; don't pursue them.
7 When your breathing is slow and relaxed, notice your heartbeat.
8 Without forcing anything, gradually try to think your heartbeat slower.
9 Next, notice the sound of your blood in your ears.
10 Without forcing anything, gradually try to think the sound slower.
11 In the same way, visit any other parts of your body that you choose.
12 Now notice the little dots that 'illuminate' the blackness of your closed eyes.
13 Imagine the dots are stars and that you're floating in an immense space inside your own body.
14 Relax your jaw and let your mouth open into a smile.
15 Continue like this as long as you like.

Tips

If you can't seem to get into a meditative state at all, try lying on the floor rather than sitting.

Try touching the tip of your ring finger against the fleshy base of your thumb as you breathe in and moving it away as you breathe out. As you breathe in think 'so' and as you breathe out think 'hum' – it's a classic mantra.

Gradually slow down your breathing, making your exhalation longer than your inhalation.

Let your mouth fall open and your tongue relax completely and drop out.

Am I meditating?

Beginners often wonder if they're meditating correctly or even at all. What should it feel like? In fact, there is no precise definition but the stages of increasingly deeper meditation should go something like this.

Stage 1. Your mind is no longer filled with everyday matters and you sense that you're drifting towards sleep; you're on the very fringe of the meditative state.

Stage 2. As you go deeper, images may come at you from nowhere. You don't actually fall asleep but start to feel as if you're floating. You may feel like rocking and swaying; that's fine at this stage but you'll need to stop moving to go deeper.

Stage 3. You become intensely aware of the functioning of your body – breathing, heartbeat, blood flow – but at the same time you no longer know where your body ends and other things begin. Parts of your body may feel very heavy.

Stage 4. You feel 'spaced out' and quite detached but, at the same time, alert.

Stage 5. You feel in touch with the universe and nothing else matters at all.

The deepest meditative states are usually only reached by those who have been practising for a long time – perhaps two or three years. But you may occasionally experience moments of those deeper states even as a beginner.

Remember this: Go with the flow

Remember that meditation is not a competition. Every experience of meditation is slightly different. Don't set out with a goal and then consider the session a failure because you didn't achieve it. Just experience and enjoy whatever occurs.

Case study: Maggie

Maggie moved to Spain to, as she puts it, 'escape the rat race'. There she joined yoga classes and one day had a particularly special experience. 'I was sitting in the half lotus at the edge of a lake. It was a beautiful, sunny, autumn day with just the lightest of winds. In front of me there were some reeds. And as I moved into a deeper state of meditation, I had the feeling I had become just like one of those reeds. I felt the warmth of the sun and the movement of the breeze and I heard the water lapping gently and the bees buzzing from flower to flower. I was almost overwhelmed by the dance of life and, like the reeds, I existed, but no more than that. I existed with no regrets, fears, hopes or desires.

CAN I LISTEN TO MUSIC?

Most music is distracting for meditation. Even if you're not consciously paying attention to it, it will sweep you away in its own rhythms. But non-melodic music is somewhat different. You may be able to find something suitably Eastern in the world music or New Age categories. There definitely shouldn't be a recognizable tune. You might also like to try sound effects – waterfalls, streams, wind, etc. If you do listen to something, play it very quietly.

> It is only in the depths of silence that the voice of God can be heard.
>
> Sai Baba (c. 1838–1918), Indian guru

Meditating for practical benefits

Above we've looked at a direct experience of inner happiness. A different style of meditation can be used in practical ways to help you create more happiness in your everyday life.

This is closer to what we might call 'having a good think'. The main difference is that you're not looking for a solution to a problem. In fact the desired outcome of your meditation is decided from the very beginning: to regain a calmer and more tranquil frame of mind regarding a difficult issue and to become happier as a result.

In other words, you're not working out how you can get even, you're not working out how you can get your own way and you're certainly not sulking. You start out knowing that the solution is not to change something in the outside world but to change something inside yourself. You meditate to find out what to change and how.

> The heart has reasons that reason knows not of.
>
> Blaise Pascal (1623–62), French philosopher

Let's take an example. Suppose a long-term relationship has ended and you have to sort out who gets what and who pays what. Unfortunately, your ex-partner is constantly angry, which makes you very upset, and you tend to respond in the same angry way. No progress is being made.

This is how you might meditate on the problem, with the aim of preserving your own happiness. It's important to stress that getting the maximum amount of money is not the object of the exercise. The way forward is to empathize with your ex-partner, that is, to put yourself in the position of your ex-partner to see how it feels, so you can behave accordingly. Let's say you were the one who broke up the relationship.

Step 1. Get yourself into a meditative state, as described earlier.

Step 2. Try to feel what your ex is feeling. It could be that he or she is thinking something like this: 'I've been rejected and that makes me feel a failure. I also feel by turns shocked, disorientated, upset, bitter, despondent and lacking in self-esteem. In order to build up my self-esteem I have to get the maximum from my ex. I'm using anger as a way of dominating the situation and getting what I want. It also helps blot out all the pain. It isn't at all easy feeling this way and when I get an angry response back it only makes me worse. If I heard some words from my ex to indicate understanding and sympathy, if my ex would just make some concessions and be conciliatory, then I'd be willing to take a softer line.'

Step 3. Visualize yourself talking together with your ex. Visualize saying different things. Which is the one that would best preserve your mental equilibrium? Given your new empathy with your ex, listen to the response your ex is likely to make to each of those different approaches.

Step 4. Visualize how you're going to feel when your ex gives those responses. Again, which is the response from your ex that's least likely to damage your happiness? Analyse what it is that's stopping you from making the approach that will make you feel happy and, hopefully, elicit the desired response from your ex.

Step 5. Visualize yourself changing your attitude to the situation and, instead, adopting an approach that will maximize happiness. Visualize yourself behaving in this new way and not allowing yourself to be deterred no matter what response your ex actually gives.

If you do this conscientiously you'll see why getting angry isn't likely to produce the happiness you want. Step 5 is very important because when it comes to the reality, your ex may not behave in the way you'd prefer. If you've already rehearsed that in your meditation you'll be prepared for it. You'll be able to deal calmly with the situation and preserve the serenity of your mind.

Key idea: Meditation is about changing yourself

It's important to repeat that the purpose of such a meditation is not how you can get your way or how you can get more, or anything like that. It's how you can change your way of looking at the situation so you can be more happy.

> You can't teach anybody anything, only make them realize the answers are already inside them.
>
> Galileo (1564–1642), Italian astronomer

Here are some other things you could meditate on:

- ▶ the good things your partner does/did for you

- ▶ the things you can be grateful for

- ▶ anger, and what it does to you

- ▶ the problems other people have in their lives

- ▶ the scale, grandeur and mystery of the universe.

Key idea: Overcoming anger

The Dalai Lama teaches several meditations for anger. One involves imagining someone you love who becomes extremely angry with you. You can see that person's face contorted with rage and it isn't nice. Now imagine that the situation is reversed and it's you who has become angry. Do you really want to be like that?

Meditating on the day's events

This is a style of meditation that's appropriate for last thing at night in bed. The idea is to review what has happened during the day and how you reacted, not in a self-critical way but in an optimistic, forward-looking sort of way. In other words, your thoughts might go something like this: 'I was a little bit brusque with someone at work; I'll put that right by making a point of being more pleasant tomorrow. I spent far too long trying to get something absolutely perfect; I now realize I wasted a lot of time so I won't do that again. My partner criticized something I'd done and instead of becoming annoyed I looked at the situation from my partner's point of view, understood, and felt much better, which resulted in a lovely evening. Good.'

Where does inner happiness come from?

So far we've talked about accessing the reservoir of inner happiness but I've said nothing about what feeds the reservoir or how you can enlarge it. In fact, it's fed by your spiritual connection with everything else in the universe. Even if you don't believe that, you can still gain tremendous benefit from meditating. So don't stop just because talk of 'spiritual' things puts you off. But if you are interested in the spiritual aspects of meditation, you'll find more in Chapter 13.

Breakthrough

Is meditation making you happier?

a Yes

b No

c At the moment I'm too busy and stressed to meditate

d You'll never catch me doing that.

If you answered 'a', you've obviously achieved a breakthrough and can move on to Chapter 8. If you answered 'b', give it more time. If you answered 'c', reflect that feeling stressed is a very good reason to meditate. Remember that meditating is not an indulgence but, among other things, can be a tool to make you more effective. Looked at like that, you can surely find 20 minutes a day in your schedule. If you answered 'd', read the chapter again. At the very worst, meditation is harmless, so what have you got to lose by trying it?

Focus points

The main points to remember from this chapter are:

* meditation is an altered state of consciousness, which occasionally occurs in daily life but normally requires focused attention
* meditation is one of the ways of accessing inner happiness
* scientists have demonstrated that meditation increases activity in the frontal lobe of the left brain – the part associated with higher moods and optimism
* meditation can give you control of your mind so unpleasant thoughts can't enter on their own
* meditation can benefit not only the mind but also the body, lowering blood pressure and boosting the immune system.

Next step

When you're meditating, as you now know, it's important to let unwanted thoughts pass through your mind like leaves blown by the wind. You're aware of them but you don't pursue them and you don't react to them. In Chapter 8, you'll learn how your whole life can be like that. It's a very different approach. Rather than fighting to change negative thoughts, as in cognitive therapy, you'll simply stand back from them and accept them without emotion – which is why it's called acceptance and commitment therapy (ACT).

8

Acceptance and commitment therapy, and mindfulness

In this chapter you will learn:

- ▶ *how to detach yourself from negative thoughts*
- ▶ *how to stop being upset by memories of the past and worries for the future*
- ▶ *how to lay down a road map for your life.*

Do not dwell in the past, do not dream of the future, concentrate the mind on the present moment.

Buddha (c.563–483 BCE), spiritual leader

Acceptance and commitment therapy (ACT) is a relatively new name in psychotherapy although the approach goes back a long way. The central idea is that, rather than fighting negative thinking (as in cognitive therapy), it's more effective (as in Buddhism's mindfulness or Smriti) to 'accept' negative thoughts but to detach yourself from them. That may not sound very much, but in the quest for happiness it can make a big difference. The other major element in ACT is the 'commitment' to actions that will improve and enrich your life – but only those that reflect your values.

It's possible you already use some ACT techniques quite naturally, without calling them by that name. Let's find out.

Self-assessment: How 'mindful' am I?

1 Someone very close to you has given their time of arrival as 11 p.m. By midnight they still haven't arrived. What do you do?

   a Leave the front door unfastened and go to bed

   b Sit up, worrying about what may have happened

   c Call the police.

2 You are mistakenly arrested on the grounds that you closely fit the description of someone who has committed a crime. What do you think?

   a This will be an extremely interesting experience which may be useful to me in some way in the future

   b As soon as this outrage is cleared up I shall sue the police for as much money as possible

   c This is a calamity – I'll probably end up in prison for a crime of which I'm innocent.

3 When you go for a walk, you:

   a observe everything very carefully

   b take the opportunity to think through your problems.

4 When you think back on mistakes you made in the past, you:

   a feel very little because, after all, it's water under the bridge.

   b relive the same emotions, although a little less intensely

5 When you feel anxious about something you want to do, you:

   a accept that worthwhile things sometimes cause anxiety

   b change your mind about doing it

   c try to talk yourself out of feeling anxious.

6 When you have something unpleasant coming up, you:

   a stay detached, neither deliberately thinking about it nor avoiding thinking about it

   b try hard not to think about it

   c prepare yourself by visualizing how it will be.

7 You have:

   a clear values which you do your best to uphold

   b clear values which sometimes have to be jettisoned

   c no clear values.

8 You have:

   a clear goals which you work towards

   b clear goals which you don't try too hard to achieve because, after all, few people can expect to succeed

   c no clear goals.

9 When something bad happens to you:

   a you shrug because, after all, into every life a little rain must fall

   b you feel bitter about the unfairness of life

   c you feel singled out to be persecuted.

10 Your philosophy is that in life you:

   a sometimes have to stand back from things

   b should always get in there and fight every step of the way.

So how did you get on? As far as ACT is concerned, you should have answered 'a' throughout. If you did answer 'a' most of the time, you're a natural at the ACT philosophy. If you answered mostly 'b' or 'c', this chapter will offer you an entirely new perspective on life.

Historical background

> Man consists of two parts, his mind and his body, only the body has more fun.
>
> Woody Allen (b. 1935), film director and comedian

There was a man, it is said, who spent 49 days meditating under a tree, seeking to know why people suffered and what could be done about it. At the end of the time, he had not found a cure for diseases, nor discovered a technology that would improve people's lives, but he nevertheless announced that he could put an end to suffering. His message was simple. Suffering is caused by a craving for worldly things. Therefore, suffering can be ended by detaching yourself from worldly things.

The man was, of course, Siddhartha Gautama, better known as the Buddha or the Enlightened One.

Very few people in the West today would wish to follow his teachings to the letter. But that's not to say he wasn't onto something.

While staying at the Anathapindika monastery at Savatthi, the Buddha is said to have explained it to his son Rahula in the following terms:

> All material forms, past, present, or future, within or without, gross or subtle, base or fine, far or near, all should be viewed with full understanding, with the thought: 'This is not mine, this is not I, this is not my soul.'

How significant this can be we'll see in a moment but, for now, let's just stick with the history of the Right Mindfulness philosophy. An equivalent philosophy can be found in Taoism (also spelt Daoism), said to have been founded by Lao Tzu (sometimes spelt Laozi) in the 6th century BCE (roughly the same time the Buddha was sitting under his tree), but with its origins stretching back much further. The great book of Taoism is Lao Tzu's *Tao Te Ching*. The central idea can be summed up in the phrases 'go with the flow' and 'let the force be with you'.

Taoism is illustrated by stories such as the following. A farmer has a horse that runs away. The villagers commiserate with the farmer because he can't plough his fields. 'What a tragedy,' they say. 'Perhaps,' he answers. A few days later the horse returns. 'What a blessing,' say the villagers. 'Perhaps,' says the farmer. The farmer's son begins ploughing a field with the horse, gets kicked, and suffers a broken leg. 'What a tragedy,' say the villagers. 'Perhaps,' says the farmer. A few days later the army comes to the village and forcibly takes the strongest young men as recruits, leaving the farmer's son because of his broken leg. 'What a blessing,' say the villagers. 'Perhaps,' says the farmer.

Remember this: Action without action

The farmer follows the Taoist principle of *wu wei* (without action). But that's not to say a Taoist never does anything positive. In fact, a better phrase is *wei wu wei* (action without action). The Taoist aims to achieve his ends working with the flow of things, rather than against them, and especially working with the flow of nature.

Mindfulness today

So how does all of this tie up with happiness? Modern psychologists have taken a look at Right Mindfulness and Taosim and developed their own version of mindfulness as a path to happiness. Psychologists being psychologists, everything is expressed in impenetrable phrases, such as relational frame theory (RFT). Rather than get bogged down in that I'm going to ask you, instead, to take part in a little experiment.

Try it now: Thinking yourself frightened

Imagine you're going to jump from a light aircraft. Do your best to visualize the whole thing. Of course, you'll be wearing a parachute. You'll climb into the aircraft through the side door and sit on the floor until it's your turn. When the aircraft reaches 12,000 feet, the other jumpers will go ahead and then it will be your turn. You'll move to the open door. You'll see the others falling away and everything on the ground will look very tiny. The combined wind and engine noise will be incredible, so the signal to jump will be given by the instructor just touching you on the shoulder. You feel the touch. You jump. Immediately the noise of the wind stops and, although you're falling fast, you hardly realize it at first. You know you have to pull the handle to open the parachute. You put your hand to where it should be but you can't find it. In panic you look up, hoping the instructor can see your plight. Big mistake! You've made yourself unstable. You start to spin... faster... and faster... and faster...

How do you feel reading that?

Is your pulse beating a little stronger? Are you experiencing any tightening across your chest? Is your stomach knotted up?

These are normal human reactions so we don't think them strange. But, when you think about it, they are strange. You're reacting not to the thing itself but to the thought of it. You probably have no intention of ever jumping out of an aircraft. And yet your mental state has been affected.

IN REAL LIFE
All day long, thoughts are coming into your head. Some are concerned with what you're doing right now, but others –

usually the majority – will consist of memories, fantasies, deductions, visualizations of the future, and so on. Some of those thoughts may be enjoyable but some of them will be unpleasant. And the unpleasant thoughts can make you feel embarrassed, anxious, fearful, low, and even depressed. In turn, those emotions can cause physical effects.

If I ask you to think about something embarrassing that happened to you in the past, then it's quite likely that your heart will beat a little faster, your stomach will churn, your palms will sweat, and so on. If I ask you to think about your visit to the dentist next week, then similarly you'll imagine being in the chair, the lights in your face, the whirring sound of the drill, the burning smell as it bores into your tooth... Once again you'll exhibit a physical reaction as if you're actually there. This is so common a human experience we simply accept it without question.

But it doesn't have to be that way.

WHY 'EXPERIENTIAL AVOIDANCE' DOESN'T WORK

'Experiential avoidance' is another one of those impenetrable phrases so loved by psychologists. It refers to the techniques we all tend to employ (in the jargon, 'emotional control strategies') to try to get rid of unpleasant thoughts, feelings, sensations, urges and memories. Some of these techniques may be harmless but many of them are not. Some people, for example, avoid social situations in which they feel and end up hardly going out at all. Some eat for comfort and become seriously overweight. Others turn to alcohol or drugs and can no longer function. So 'experiential avoidance' can actually cause worse problems than it solves. In fact, it may not solve any problems at all because, sooner or later, these techniques tend to stop working.

Keep smiling

> Not everyone who drinks is a poet. Some of us drink because we're not poets.
>
> > Dudley Moore (1935–2002), actor and comedian

Try it now: Evaluate your existing strategy

Make a list of all the 'emotional control strategies' you use. For each of them ask yourself the following questions.

* Has this strategy reduced my symptoms in the long term?
* What has this strategy cost me in terms of time, energy, health and relationships?
* Has this strategy brought me closer to the life I want?

If you conclude that your strategies don't work, or if you conclude they have too high a cost, you may find ACT is the way forward.

Key idea: Don't torture yourself

ACT professionals sometimes make a distinction between things that are 'clean' and things that are 'dirty'; for example, between 'clean pain' and 'dirty pain'. 'Clean pain' is the normal, straightforward experience of something physically or emotionally damaging. 'Dirty pain' is the pain people create through inappropriate ways of trying to avoid the 'clean pain'. Some people, for example, dwell at length on potential disasters as a defence mechanism in case a real disaster should occur. This self-inflicted suffering is 'dirty pain'.

Why do these emotional control strategies so often fail? The devices you use to distract yourself can, through relational framing, themselves become reminders of the very thing you're trying to avoid. Let's say you drink alcohol to forget some unpleasant memory. Initially it might work. But because of the human ability to create these relationships, a bottle of alcohol will itself become something that symbolizes the unpleasant memory. So each time you reach for the bottle to forget, say, that you've been made redundant, you actually remind yourself of that very thing.

It gets worse. Let's say that heights cause you to have feelings of panic, which manifest as a pounding heart. Therefore you avoid heights. Seeing an attractive member of the opposite sex also causes a pounding heart. Because of this ability to create 'frames of coordination', some people will now also feel panic when they see an attractive member of the opposite sex. Perhaps being given a present causes a pounding heart. So now getting a present causes panic. And so it goes on. Of course, this is an extreme example for the purpose of illustration. But you can see how, if you're unlucky, everything can get tangled up in this way.

This is where mindfulness comes in.

Key idea: The quicksand

Imagine you've stepped into quicksand. You struggle to get out. But those very struggles actually cause you to sink deeper and deeper. The only way to survive the quicksand is to accept it. Instead of struggling you relax and lie down on it. As a result you float on the top and can make your way to firm ground. It's the same with negative thoughts. Don't struggle with them. Just accept them and relax.

Keep smiling

> One reason I don't drink is that I want to know when I am having a good time.
>
> Nancy Astor (1879 –1964), first British woman
> MP to sit in the House of Commons

MINDFULNESS IN PRACTICE

Essentially, modern mindfulness is an 'emotional control strategy' that avoids damaging side effects. There are three parts to it:

▶ focusing on the present moment with an attitude of openness and curiosity

▶ acceptance of painful feelings, urges and sensations, allowing them to come and go

▶ defusion, that is, distancing from negative thoughts.

Let's start with focusing on the present moment. Why should this promote happiness? Well, if you're the sort of person who is always ruminating on things that went wrong in the past, or who is always anticipating problems that might occur in the future, then mindfulness will relieve you of a considerable burden. What's more, paying attention to the present moment means you live life more fully.

Try it now: Savour life

Find something to drink (it could be a glass of wine, a cup of tea or a glass of water). Also find something simple to eat (for example, a few olives, a piece of bread or an apple). Take a gulp of whatever you're drinking and swallow it immediately. Similarly, take a bite of your snack and swallow it at once. After a pause, again take a mouthful of your drink but this time roll it around your tongue, savour it, try to describe the flavour or flavours, and let it trickle a little at a time down your throat. Similarly, take a bite of your snack, chew it carefully, move it around your mouth, identify the flavour or flavours, and only then swallow it.

This is the difference between non-mindfulness and mindfulness. Without mindfulness you get very little out of your experiences.

Life is colourless and unsatisfying. Things happen but you hardly remember them because you never really experienced them in the first place. With mindfulness, everything becomes more interesting, more satisfying and more powerful.

So by focusing on the present, you crowd out upsetting memories, projections and fantasies. By being totally absorbed in what you're seeing and doing now, you have no opportunity to be gloomy.

But what about when the present moment itself isn't very nice? What about when, say, you're having a tooth filled? Do you really want to be mindful of that? In fact, in most situations there are still interesting things you can focus on. Maybe the background music, the tools the dentist is using, the dentist's hands, the chair.

Remember this: Quality not quantity

It isn't necessary to have lots of different things to do. 'Focusing on the present' doesn't require that. On the contrary, you could just sit quietly watching clouds pass by.

Try it now: Less emotional involvement

Imagine you're a journalist on the lookout for a good story. The very next unpleasant situation you're involved in will provide you with one. Contemplate the situation with the eye of a journalist, taking careful note of exactly what's happening and the details that will bring the whole experience to life. Write the opening sentences of your report in your head. By focusing objectively on the present moment in this way you should find your personal emotions take a back seat.

Remember this: You can still daydream

Of course you should not completely deny yourself the pleasure of reliving joyful past events, of looking forward to future events or of creating gorgeous fantasies. Thinking about something pleasurable activates the mesolimbic dopamine system in the brain almost as much as actually doing the thing. So carry on with your happy recollections, projections and daydreams – the day you fell in love, a forthcoming holiday, perhaps an exciting fantasy about yourself and someone you're attracted to. But these kinds of thoughts should be a much smaller percentage of your mental life than they probably are now. And when it comes to upsetting memories, projections and fantasies, use the technique of focusing on the present to reduce them to almost nothing.

Try it now: Mindfulness by the clock

Think of something that will automatically jog your memory several times a day. It could be passing through a particular doorway, for example, or having a cup of coffee. If nothing springs to mind, simply set your watch or mobile phone to alert you once an hour. Whatever the signal, when you get it, check whether or not you're 'in the present moment'. If you're not, put your thoughts on pause and spend five minutes fully exploring everything around you using all of your senses. Keep on with this technique until mindfulness has become a habit.

Key idea: Mindfulness makes memories

Think back to your last holiday. How much of it can you remember? Which bits? Almost certainly you'll remember best the most dramatic, exciting or frightening times because those are the ones that will have forced you to be the most mindful. That means that when you're not mindful you don't remember so well – and your past life is lost as if it had never happened.

ACCEPTANCE IN PRACTICE

Now let's turn to the second ingredient in mindfulness, acceptance, and see what it really means.

Some youngsters on a school trip are asked to do something a bit scary. Let's say abseiling down a cliff. Feeling anxious, one of them tries to get out of it. He says he suffers from a fear of heights and the instructor excuses him. In fact, all the others also feel anxious. But they accept their emotions as part of the whole experience. They complete the abseil and afterwards feel both elated and more self-confident. By contrast, the boy who didn't abseil feels both left out and diminished.

The lessons of this story are these. First, it isn't that some people feel anxiety and some don't, or that some people feel fear and some don't. It's that some people accept the feeling of anxiety, or fear, but carry on doing what they want anyway. The second point is that the boy who refused to abseil learned nothing either about abseiling or about conquering his own mind.

Remember this: Ignore the fear and do it

Feelings of apprehension, anxiety, fear, etc. are just that – feelings. The feelings themselves can't hurt you.

Try it now: Analyse anxiety

Visualize yourself in a situation that makes you anxious. Where does that anxiety manifest itself? Perhaps in your stomach? Now imagine being a scientist who is fascinated by the physical manifestation of this anxiety. In the role of scientist, measure the area affected by the anxiety and make frequent observations to note whether it grows or diminishes, whether it pulsates or remains constant, whether it generates heat or cold, and so on. The idea is to think of anxiety as an interesting phenomenon and not to be intimidated by it.

DEFUSION IN PRACTICE

'Defusion' is a bit of ACT jargon. What we're actually talking about is *defusing* negative thoughts by creating a distance between 'you' and those thoughts.

Try it now: The real you

Close your eyes and observe your thoughts. Do they take any particular form, position or colour? If you can observe them, there must be, as it were, an 'observing self'. The ACT view is that you are not your physical body, thoughts, emotions, urges or memories. They are associated with you but they're not you. You are something unchanging, ever-present and impervious to harm.

Here's a key question. Do you talk to yourself, either out loud or internally? Of course you do. But in that case, who is talking to whom? In fact, we all have this concept of being almost two people. One 'you' does things and the other 'you' observes and comments: 'You can do it', 'You made a mess of that', 'How many times have I told you not to forget the keys'. And so on.

Defusion increases the distance between the doing 'you' and the observing 'you'.

An analogy is that you're looking at yourself in the same way that a naturalist looks at nature. A naturalist doesn't judge some animals as 'bad' because they're predators or as 'good' because they only eat plants. A naturalist doesn't get emotionally involved. A naturalist simply observes, accepting the way the natural world is, and goes home afterwards. In the same way, when you observe yourself, you should strive to have the naturalist's detachment.

Try it now: Distance yourself

Recall an upsetting thought you sometimes have, such as 'I'm a failure' or 'I'm a rotten mother'. Note how that makes you feel. Now try putting these words in front: 'I'm having the thought that…'. Now how do you feel?

The idea is to help you realize that a thought is just a thought. It isn't the thing itself and it may not be an accurate assessment anyway.

Another technique is to take a negative phrase that bothers you (such as 'No one likes me') and try to see it in different ways. Again, the idea is to help you realize that these are just words, not reality. So visualize the words in front of you and try changing the colour, the size, the typeface and the position. Then set fire to them or pour acid over them and watch them disappear. You see, they have no substance at all.

Case study: Rita

Ever since she was a young woman Rita had been very used to making speeches. Highly sociable, she had been a member of all kinds of organizations, had been on committees and had been chairperson many times. But after retiring from her job she began to find public speaking increasingly intimidating. The night before a meeting she could hardly sleep for worrying about it, and as she waited for her name to be called her heart would pound so hard that she feared it would explode. She tried all kinds of therapies, including CT and NLP, but none worked for her. Then a friend recommended an ACT practitioner. Rather than getting her to combat negative thoughts, as in CT, or to visualize a successful speech, as in NLP, he taught her to stop visualizing anything to do with the speech at all. Instead she was to live more in the present moment and to accept any anxious thoughts that entered her mind as if she were watching twigs float past on a stream. Rita found this new approach suited her and is once again chairperson of her local women's group.

Keep smiling

Life is full of misery, loneliness and suffering – and it's all over much too soon.

Woody Allen (b. 1935), film director and comedian

The commitment bit

There are two core processes we haven't yet discussed:

▶ values – what you want your life to be about, what you want to do on the planet, what you want to be remembered for

▶ committed action – taking action guided by your values.

ACT places great emphasis not just on action but on action consistent with values. It's a prerequisite, therefore, that you should be clear what your values are. Not everyone is. If you've never sat down and thought about it, or if you have no kind of 'road map' for your life, no goals, no ambitions for how you'd like things to be in, say, five years' time, the following exercise could be something of a revelation.

Try it now: Write about your dreams

What I want you to do is write a little about your values with regard to the following key subjects. There's no time limit. You don't have to answer the specific questions – they're just to provoke some ideas. If you can't think of anything to write under a particular heading, spend a few days mulling it over and then try again. It's very important that while completing this exercise you should be:

✳ completely honest – set down your genuine feelings, not the feelings you think you 'should' have

✳ ambitious – set down your wildest dreams; don't tone things down to what seems attainable.

Remember, the object of the exercise is not to write about the values an ideal person would have, but about the ideals you actually have.

1 My partner. What sort of person would you really like to be with your partner? What kind of relationship would you really like to have? Would you like to be more entertaining? Less irritable? Sexier? Would you want to be together more of the time or would you want to be freer to pursue your personal interests?

2 My family. How would you be if you were an ideal father/mother, son/daughter, brother/sister, etc? Remember, we're

not concerned with the ideal from the other person's point of view but from your point of view. (So don't say, for example, you'd like to spend more time helping your grandparents if that's not genuinely what you want.)

3 My friends. Are friends important to you? How much time do you want to spend with friends? What sort of friend would you want to be to them? Would you like to be more supportive or do you find friends too demanding?

4 The world. Do you feel you want to make the world a better place? If so, in what ways? Why do you feel as you do?

5 My education. Are you still in education? Would you like to return to education? What would you ideally want to study? Why?

6 My work. What work would you ideally want to do? Why? What, for you, is the goal of working? What sort of relationship would you want with your employer? With your colleagues? How important is money?

7 My leisure. What would you ideally want to do with your leisure time? Would you like to have more leisure time? What qualities would you like to bring to your leisure pursuits?

8 My health. Is your health important to you? If so, do you follow advice on nutrition, alcohol, smoking, exercise, and so on? If not, why not?

9 My rules. Do you observe certain rules of behaviour? For example, would you steal if you thought you could get away with it? If you have rules, where do they come from? Have you reviewed them recently?

10 My spiritual beliefs. Do you believe in God? If so, is religion important to you? If you're an atheist, do you nevertheless place importance on spiritual values? If so, what are they? Do you believe your life has a meaning? If so, do you know what it is? Or do you believe the universe is random? If so, do you want to give your life a meaning? What would that meaning be?

Once you've completed writing about your values, try to get the things you want to do into some sort of order of importance. For example, if you want to spend more time climbing the world's major peaks but also want to spend more time with your partner (who doesn't like climbing), which is going to take priority?

Now what? In fact, the very act of making the list is quite important in itself. Sander Thomaes of the Department of Psychology at Utrecht University asked a group of adolescents to write about their positive traits and skills on two occasions six weeks apart. After another six weeks this group was found to be more helpful and cooperative than a control group, with the biggest impact occurring among adolescents who had previously exhibited antisocial tendencies. It's believed the stronger sense of identity created by the exercise made them less susceptible to pressure from other unruly teens.

But you're going to try to take things much further than that. You're going to try to make your dreams come true. For a week read through what you've written every day. After that, refer to what you've written at least once a week and whenever you feel you need guidance about how you should act.

Case study: Tom

Tom had always been a bit of a rebel at school, campaigning on issues from poverty in Africa to overfishing in the North Sea. But when he left school he went straight into the family fashion business, just as he was expected to. It all seemed so right. Within a year he was driving around in his own sports car and within two years he was buying his own flat. There was just one problem. He had no interest in clothes and he wasn't happy. Then he began going out with Anna, who worked for a charity defending human rights around the world. His idealism fired once again, Tom was torn between two different worlds, became depressed and consulted a psychotherapist. She set him the values exercise you've just done. Today, Tom works for the same charity as Anna. He had to sell the sports car but, with their joint incomes, there's still the flat. And if you ask him, he'll tell you he's far happier than he ever was in the fashion business.

Breakthrough

Are you giving up harmful emotional control strategies (such as drunkenness, tobacco, recreational drugs, comfort eating or the avoidance of situations that create anxiety) and using mindfulness instead?

a Yes

b No.

If you answered 'a', congratulations on breaking through one of the most difficult barriers of all. Giving up a crutch and learning to walk unaided is never easy. If you answered 'b', read this chapter again and spend some time reflecting on it. It may be that an emotional control strategy is damaging, say, your health, your relationships or your work. If it's harming your ability to achieve what you want, either in the short term or in the long term, then it's counterproductive and the answer is clear. Research shows that we all tend to ignore information or advice that we'd prefer not to hear. Think about it.

Focus points

The main points to remember from this chapter are:

* according to acceptance and commitment therapy (ACT), fighting against negative thoughts can sometimes cause more problems than it solves
* the ACT solution is mindfulness
* mindfulness involves living much more in the present moment
* mindfulness also involves accepting negative thoughts and emotions but detaching from them
* it's important to commit yourself to your goals but you must always act in accordance with your values.

Keep smiling

> How many psychologists does it take to change a light bulb?
> None – the light bulb will change itself when it's ready.

> However many holy words you read, however many you
> speak, what good will they do you if you do not act upon
> them?
>
> Buddha (c.563–483 BCE), spiritual leader

Next step

So you now know what your values are, and you
know that anxiety is the price you sometimes
have to pay when you put your values at the
forefront of your life. In Chapter 9, you'll be
pursuing this theme further, delving more deeply
into who you really are and learning how to do
exactly what you want.

9

Be who you are, do what you want

In this chapter you will learn:

- ▶ *how to achieve the maximum satisfaction of your whole being*
- ▶ *why you should be a hedonist*
- ▶ *how you can run away to happiness.*

Life isn't about finding yourself. Life is about creating yourself.

George Bernard Shaw (1856–1950), Irish dramatist

The summit of happiness is reached when a person is ready to be what he is.

Erasmus (c.1466–1536), Dutch scholar

When asked what makes them happy, most people's immediate reaction is to mention very tangible things. Sometimes they're 'big' things like houses and cars; more often they're 'small' things like hearing their children laugh. But one issue comes up again and again: people are unhappy when they feel they're constrained and happy when they feel free to be themselves.

So let's see how free you are.

Self-assessment: How free am I?

For each of the following pairs of sentences, select the one that is closest to your view:

1

   a I do what I want to do and don't worry about what other people think.

   b I would feel very uncomfortable doing anything other people disapproved of.

2

   a I don't worry too much about what other people think of me.

   b What other people think of me is very important.

3

   a I've made a few mistakes but that's normal – I don't give myself a hard time.

   b The mistakes I've made have been quite intolerable.

4

    a All things considered, I'm pretty happy being me.

    b I wish I could be more like my heroes and a bit less like me.

5

    a I've tried living in various different kinds of places.

    b I've always lived in the same place.

6

    a I've tried various kinds of jobs.

    b I've always had the same job.

7

    a My clothing, my appearance, my home and my possessions all reflect the real me.

    b In everything I do, I always try my best to conform.

8

    a I spend a great deal of time doing things that bring me the maximum possible satisfaction.

    b I spend a lot of time doing the things I should, even though I don't enjoy them.

9

    a Running away from things that are unpleasant or frightening is the rational thing to do.

    b It's cowardly to run away from things that are unpleasant or frightening.

10

    a I feel free to be myself.

    b I feel I can't be myself.

The real you

If you can't be yourself, you can't be happy. That's clear from what people say in surveys. You probably know it from your own life because very few of us are fortunate enough to be entirely 'happy in our own skins'. There's always something we're frightened of showing to the world. It can be for various reasons. It may be that we had overbearing, over-ambitious, controlling parents and are now too inhibited to reveal ourselves. It may be that the people who surround us are repressing us in some way.

George Bernard Shaw and Erasmus, quoted above, approached the question of who you are from different directions. The famous playwright was a man with little formal schooling who educated himself in the British Museum reading room. No wonder he saw himself as self-created. Erasmus, who had a long formal education, saw identity more as something inherent which needs to be discovered.

The latest research suggests that Erasmus was closer to the truth. The key question George Bernard Shaw needed to ask himself was what drove him to spend so much time in the reading room. Much of what makes us the way we are is down to our genes. More specifically, the differences between people's personality traits are roughly 50 per cent heritable. This may be either good news or bad news, depending on which traits you happen to have inherited. The particularly good news is that there is a 'real you' pretty much fixed by your genes. Although it seems we might be able to turn certain genes on or off, with present technology it's fair to say that, by and large, fate dealt you cards that can't be changed. You never were an entirely blank slate for other people to write on; there truly is an essence to be discovered. And that's important because if you're not very happy now, unleashing the real you could make a big difference.

Let's say you inherited a tendency to be very open to new ideas and experiences but have always been trapped in a narrow-minded milieu. Or let's say you're genetically primed to be introverted but have a pushy mother who is always forcing you into the limelight. Or let's say you just never had the opportunity to explore the kinds of excitement that your genes incline you to. Then uncovering the 'genetic you' and giving it full expression could make a huge difference to your happiness.

Maximum satisfaction

> The shift comes about when we seriously ask ourselves: in what situation do I experience the maximum satisfaction of my whole being?

> Arne Naess (1912–2009), Norwegian ecologist and philosopher

Making up your mind to be what you want and do what you want is only the beginning of the solution. Because you now have to find out what it is that you want. You might think you know. But you could easily be mistaken.

The Norwegian philosopher and 'deep ecologist' Arne Naess advised that we should each ask ourselves: 'In what situation do I experience the maximum satisfaction of my whole being?' This is far more profound than it first seems. Think about it: the maximum satisfaction; your whole being. Suddenly, things like watching television and shopping go straight out the window. We're looking for things that are more fundamental and profound. More real.

Key idea: Only you can know

So what are the things that give you the maximum satisfaction? What makes you feel physically, mentally and spiritually alive to the ultimate degree? Only you can answer that. Nobody else.

Try it now: Record your hours of maximum satisfaction

If you think you know the things that cause you to 'experience the maximum satisfaction', then write down the number of hours a week you spend on those things. For example, your list might start like this:

Things that give 'maximum satisfaction'	Hours a week
Playing with my children	4
Making love with my partner	1
Hillwalking	2

When you've done that, make a second list of all the other things you do, the things that don't give much satisfaction: the chores, the routines, the boring minutiae of existence. It might start like this:

Things that give 'minimum satisfaction'	Hours a week
Cooking and washing up	44
Commuting to work	15

Now compare the two lists. In all probability, you'll find you're spending at least six hours doing 'boring', 'minimal satisfaction' things for every hour of 'maximum satisfaction' things. It could even be that you've never yet experienced 'maximum satisfaction'.

Don't assume that life has to be that way. Just because thousands of other people commute long distances to work doesn't mean you have to. Just because thousands of other people do jobs they don't enjoy doesn't mean you have to. Just because thousands of other people live somewhere boring doesn't mean you have to.

Remember this: Now increase those hours

If the list you've just compiled is going to be more than an entertaining experiment, you've got to make up your mind to take control of your life. You've got to be absolutely determined to increase the amount of time you spend on the 'maximum satisfaction' things and reduce the amount of time you spend on the 'minimum satisfaction' things.

Be a hedonist

We had been taking t'ai chi lessons for about three months when my partner and I decided we were going to 'drop out', 'downsize' and move from south-east England to the Pyrenees. When we told our instructor he gave us a disapproving look and announced: 'It's easy to be happy in the mountains. The trick is to be happy in the town.' He obviously disapproved of us trying to find what he saw as an 'easy' solution by getting out of the daily commute.

That set me thinking. No doubt there are some very extraordinary people who can be happy in the direst situations or places. But can we be expected to emulate them? In my opinion, no. They rank alongside gurus who can control their heartbeats, who have learned to keep their bodies hot sitting almost naked in the snow, or who can skewer their tongues without feeling pain. Incredible they may be but those things are not for you or me. We're never going to attain that level so there's no point in building our personal philosophies around the attempt.

WHY NOT TAKE THE EASY WAY?

Of course, not everyone sees the town as a difficult place to be happy. On the contrary, many people love city life. That's fine. The important thing is to live the life that's right for you. As it turned out, the little village in the mountains posed challenges of its own but it was right for us and, in that sense, it was easy. It made us happy. For you it may not be the Pyrenees. It could be Peterborough or Pittsburgh or Palma. The important thing is for you to discover the way of life that makes you happy and then to pursue it.

TO BE A HEDONIST

The word 'hedonism' comes from the ancient Greek for pleasure. Hedonism gets a bad press. There's an automatic assumption that people who pursue pleasure are selfish, greedy and immoral. Well, they might be. But they don't have to be. You can be a hedonist and ethical at the same time. Ethical hedonism is the idea that all people have the right to do everything in their power to achieve the greatest amount of pleasure possible to them, assuming that their actions do not infringe on the equal rights of others. As a philosophical concept it goes back more than two thousand years to Aristippus of Cyrene.

But various other philosophers have argued that hedonism is bound to fail. The psychiatrist Viktor Frankl wrote in his book *Man's Search For Meaning* that: 'Happiness cannot be pursued; it must ensue, and it only does so as the unintended side effect of one's personal dedication to a cause greater than oneself or as the by-product of one's surrender to a person other than oneself.'

I wouldn't disagree that working for a cause you believe in can be a significant source of happiness. As to surrendering to another person, I'm not sure what Frankl had in mind. But I'm quite certain that these are not the 'only' ways of finding happiness, as Frankl believed. Like so many of us, Frankl had a puritannical streak that coloured his judgement.

But if there's nothing wrong with the pursuit of pleasure why do we instinctively feel that there is? The answer to that lies in natural selection. Consider the experiments on rats conducted by James Olds and Peter Milner. The rats had electrodes implanted in the pleasure centres of their brains and by pressing a lever they could turn on the current and create a state of ecstasy. The result? They carried on pressing, neither stopping to eat or drink, till exhaustion. Obviously, any creatures that carried on like that in the wilds would have succumbed to predators very quickly. So throughout evolution hedonism was deselected. But we're not rats and we're unlikely to be eaten alive while in the pursuit of pleasure. All those negative feelings are redundant. So go ahead. Indulge yourself.

But in what?

RUNNING AWAY TO HAPPINESS

> One Law for the Lion & Ox is Oppression.
>
>> William Blake (1757–1827), English poet and mystic

From early childhood we're usually told we mustn't run away from things. It's also the message of countless books and films.

The hero is a man or woman who stands up against all odds. Well, that's fine in fiction. But real life is different. If you want to be happy you have to learn not only that you can run away but that sometimes you must run away. Otherwise you're stuck with situations in which you arrived through somebody else's choice, through your own ignorance or simply by accident. So run away and be proud of it because it's the rational thing to do.

When you're young and inexperienced, you can't know what makes you happy. You can't know if you're a lion or an ox. That's something you can only find out from trial and error.

If you don't learn to run away then, you're going to be stuck with the very first thing you try. You're going to be lumbered with the first girl or boy you ever go out with, the first employer who ever takes you on and the first town you ever decide to live in.

What's more – and this is very important – you can't even know what things you might like to try. It's possible that the very thing that could make you happy is something you haven't even heard of yet. But while you're running, you'll encounter all kinds of new situations, and one day you'll find, perhaps purely by chance, the one that really makes you happy.

Let's try to define what's meant by 'running away' here. It doesn't mean leaving home at 15 years old without telling anybody. It doesn't mean dumping your wife and children without support. It doesn't mean leaving work without giving notice. But it is the very opposite of that old-fashioned advice: 'You've made your bed and now you've got to lie in it.' You haven't got to lie in it. In fact, if you're not happy, it would be better for everybody if you found another 'bed'. Here's why.

▶ If you're not very good at your job (because it's not what you really want to do), then it's not just you that's suffering. It's also the company and your fellow employees. If you change to a job you do like, everyone will benefit.

▶ If you're not actually in love with your partner, then it's not just you that's suffering. He/she is suffering as well. A separation/divorce will give you both the chance to find true love.

▶ If you're not happy with your university course, then it's not just you that's suffering. It's your tutor, the university and the taxpayer too. Changing to the right course is in everyone's interests.

Of course, some people are happy with the cards that fate has dealt them. You're almost bound to feel comfortable in the place you were brought up. The landscape, the buildings, the climate, the way people dress and talk and behave will all be familiar. Somehow they'll probably seem 'right' precisely because you're used to them. That's why so many people insist: 'My country is the best country in the world.'

But not every country can be the 'best country in the world'. Isn't it more sensible to try a few before deciding? And for 'country' you can substitute town, job, hobby and plenty of other things.

> Twenty years from now you will be more disappointed by the things you didn't do than by the ones you did do. So throw off the bowlines. Sail away from the safe harbour. Catch the trade winds in your sails. Explore. Dream. Discover.
>
> Mark Twain (1835–1910), American writer

Try it now: Be curious

While you're 'running away', don't run so fast that you haven't got time to enjoy everything you pass. The more things you take an interest in, the more possibilities you have for being happy.

So, for today, show an interest in everything. When you see a flower, stop and count the petals and take careful note of the colour of the stamens (the male bits that produce the pollen). When you pass a tree, stop and take careful note of the bark; touch it with your hand. Whenever you meet anyone, find out something about them. When you're confronted with a piece of equipment, find out how it works.

RUNNING AWAY TO THE SUNSHINE

Quite a lot of people in northern latitudes dream of running away to the sunshine. Perhaps you're one of them. It makes good sense if you're one of those people who feel low in winter. Some bodies just don't work very well when there's too little daylight. Lack of light causes a reduction in serotonin (a neurotransmitter that helps us to feel happy) and an increase in melatonin (which makes us sleepy). It's a condition known as seasonal affective disorder (SAD).

There are three possible solutions.

1 To learn to be happy despite the lack of sunlight.

2 To enjoy 'artificial sunlight' every day in winter.

3 To move somewhere with more sunshine in winter.

Don't forget that if you're British or a citizen of a member state of the European Union, you have the right to live and work in most other member states. So if it's sunshine you want and need, nobody can stop you going to find it in Portugal, Spain (including the Canary Islands, which are only just outside the tropics), the south of France, Italy or Malta, to name a few places. Don't think only in terms of the coast. You'll also find plenty of sunshine in winter at altitude in the Pyrenees and the Alps – at 1,000 metres or more, you'll often be above the clouds while everyone at lower altitudes suffers. Of course, it won't be hot up a mountain in winter but that doesn't matter where SAD is concerned.

If you're a US citizen, you have the right to live almost as far south as the Tropic of Cancer.

Millions of people have already done it. Why not you?

But if you can't move for some reason, you can get some of the benefits of sunlight artificially by using a special SAD lightbox. Here's an idea of the light intensities:

▶ typical home or office lighting – 200–500 lux

▶ cheap SAD lightbox – 2,500 lux

▶ top-of-the-range SAD lightbox – 10,000 lux

▶ bright summer's day – 100,000 lux.

Obviously, a light box that emits 10,000 lux will be effective in a much shorter time than one that emits 2,500 lux (say,

30 minutes a session rather than two hours). So it makes sense to get the best you can afford. You can get on with other things while you're receiving the light therapy. Just sit close to it while you're having a meal, reading or doing some office jobs, for example. (Note that you shouldn't look directly at the light.) So, if you have the opportunity to be by your lightbox for two hours every day, the highest power may not be vital in your case.

Doing what you want

> If there is a path it is someone else's path and you are not on the adventure.
>
> Joseph Campbell (1904–87), American writer

In our lives we are often advised to follow the path less travelled. But Joseph Campbell was right; even that's not good enough. Whenever you follow an existing path, you're not being yourself. You should aim to make your own path. If that happens to be very similar to many other paths, that's fine. But if, like the starship *Enterprise*, you want to go where no man [or woman] has gone before, don't be put off. You don't have to be afraid of being different. The important point is that it's the path you want. Not a path someone else has told you to follow.

> Sooner murder an infant in its cradle than nurse unacted desires.
>
> William Blake (1757–1827), English poet and mystic

Ask yourself how often things you've done have made you unhappy. Now ask yourself how often you've been unhappy because you didn't do something you wanted to do. In all probability you will think of ten times more of the latter than the former. The fact is that it's what we don't do that usually makes us most unhappy. It's the person we didn't ask out, the time we didn't say 'I love you', the exam we didn't study for, the travel opportunity we didn't take, the job we didn't apply for, and so on.

This is the meaning of Blake's proverb. He's not actually suggesting anyone should murder a baby. In fact, the baby in the proverb is you. Blake is saying that if you don't do the things you want to do in life, it's as if you'd been murdered as a baby. You're not fulfilling your promise. You're not becoming what you could have become. The person you should have been is effectively dead. Murdered.

> **Remember this:** Conventional is fine, too
>
> Remember that Blake was writing about 'unacted desires'. You don't have to do something you don't want to do because you're afraid other people will think you're too conventional. It's fine to be conventional – just as long as you're sure that you are.

Say 'yes' to variety

> But if a man doesn't break the string, tell me, what flavour is left in life? You're young, you have money, health, you're a good fellow, you lack nothing. Nothing, by thunder! Except just one thing – folly!

Nikos Kazantzakis (1883–1957), author of *Zorba the Greek*

It's very easy to say 'no'. And sometimes, of course, very necessary and sensible. When you say 'no', you can usually predict the outcome with certainty. 'No' means that everything stays as it is. So 'no' is the safe option.

But sometimes it's far more interesting to take the unsafe option and say 'yes'. When you say 'yes', you embark on a journey whose outcome is unknown.

Of course, we have to get this business of 'no' and 'yes' into perspective. There are many things to which we must say 'no'. But some people say 'no' to almost anything that's new. They say 'no' to whatever threatens to disturb their routine and their security, 'no' to new ideas, 'no' to new situations. If you were absolutely positive that the status quo is exactly what you want, you probably wouldn't be reading this book. The fact is that lots of people say 'no' but regret it afterwards.

Research shows that sticking to the familiar is not a recipe for happiness. This is due to 'hedonic adaptation'. We come to accept things as normal and no longer notice them, no matter how pleasurable they were to begin with. We need the stimulation of the new. There are certainly some important exceptions to this, but as a broad principle it holds good.

So it turns out that variety is not only the spice of life, it's also an important source of happiness. Of course, no one is suggesting everything has to be varied. For most people there has to be a stable foundation to life. But in certain things it is variety that gets the dopamine flowing and gives life its sparkle.

The obvious course, then, is to keep saying 'yes' to new experiences. But, intriguingly, there's one additional factor to take into account. A research team headed by Sonja Lyubomirsky concluded that the right timing is also vital. She found, for example, that a person performing five different acts of kindness in one day derived more long-lasting happiness than if the kind acts were spread out over the week. We'll be looking at kindness as a source of happiness in a later chapter, but meanwhile the message is to experiment with the frequency of new things to see what works best for you.

Case study: Samantha and Tim

Samantha and Tim met when they were in their early thirties. Sam ran her own very successful business and Tim had a well-paid job in the City of London. People envied them and yet neither felt truly fulfilled. As they tentatively began to reveal their dreams to each other, they realized they were kindred spirits and drew confidence from one another, developing ideas that were further and further 'out of the box'. Within a few months they'd sold or given away almost everything they owned – the business, homes, cars, personal possessions. Part of the money was put safely into interest-bearing investments and the rest went into their 'see-the-world' fund. In the first year they lived with near-naked islanders in the Pacific, studied Tantra in India, trekked through Mongolia, and much else. In most of the places they travelled to, they found somewhere to stay for free in exchange for a little work. And so they kept going, living on a shoestring with no place to call home.

I met them six years after they first set out and seldom have I encountered two such carefree, happy, optimistic people. Never had they come close to settling down because, as they told me, 'there's always another beautiful place to see'. They have no plans to ever live differently. It's not a life for everyone, probably very few, but their story illustrates something universal. If you have a dream that's unconventional, don't let that put you off. If you want to be happy, then, whatever your dream, you must follow it.

Keep smiling

I don't suffer from insanity, I enjoy every minute of it.

Try it now: How daring are you?

If the following suggestions were made to you, what would you answer? Yes or no?

✻ Let's go on holiday to a country we've never visited before.
✻ Let's sell up and move to a new country.
✻ Let's live on a boat.
✻ Let's get backpacks/a motorbike and travel round the world.
✻ Let's build our own house, exactly as we want it.
✻ Let's make love in a position we've never tried before.
✻ Let's find jobs/work doing the things we really want to do.
✻ Let's give up our jobs and start our own business.
✻ Let's have makeovers and completely change the way we look.
✻ Let's take up an adrenaline sport.
✻ Let's go to evening classes to learn a new skill.
✻ Let's adopt orphans/take in refugees.

There are 12 suggestions here. How many would you be willing to consider? Before you answer, let's take a look at the true story of Richard.

Case study: Richard

Following his divorce, a horse trainer called Richard bought some land in the middle of nowhere on which he intended to live in a mobile home and lick his wounds, far from everyone. That was the plan. Today, he heads a charitable foundation that, in the peace and quiet of the countryside, helps people who've been traumatized. This dramatic change came about because Richard said 'yes'. He said 'yes' to a woman he met by chance who told him his land was far too beautiful for him to keep all to himself. She suggested that he 'shared' it. And that's what he did. Using horses, he helps diagnose and treat people who are troubled and depressed – a fascinating new approach known as equitherapy.

Today, Richard is a happy man – a very happy man. He could easily have said 'no'. Most people would have done. But he was curious to know what would happen if he said 'yes'.

> Security is mostly a superstition. It does not exist in nature, nor do children of men as a whole experience it. Avoiding danger is no safer in the long run than outright exposure. Life is either a daring adventure, or nothing.
>
> Helen Keller (1880–1968), American campaigner for the blind

So back to those questions. To how many would you answer 'yes'? Ten? Then you're obviously very adventurous and optimistic. And a bit wild. You take risks and things sometimes go wrong but you probably don't mind. Five? You're certainly open to new ideas but you like to weigh them up before you act. Two? One? None? Then you need to ask yourself, are you simply very fortunate and contented or are you, perhaps, afraid of life?

These are big things. But, so often, happiness comes from seemingly little things. It could come when you're hosing the flowers and you get the urge to spray your partner instead. It could come at a dinner party when you get the urge to make a controversial remark or tell a particularly risqué joke. It could come when you're on a deserted beach and you get the urge to throw off your clothes and swim naked. It could come at a social gathering when you get the urge to put your arms round the two nearest guests and sing a song.

The seemingly little things are often the ones to do with the most profound issues of the human spirit. They're to do with inhibition and liberation. They're to do with being yourself, with self-expression, with being comfortable in your own skin. Find time for them.

There's a lovely scene in the 1989 movie *Shirley Valentine* in which, while decorating a room, Shirley and her husband (played by Pauline Collins and Bernard Hill) end up happily slapping paint on one another. It's a tiny moment in their relationship when they're suddenly free – perhaps it was the only one in their entire lives together.

Of course, there are many laws, rules, conventions and manners we have to observe if we're going to live alongside other people. Even, indeed, to live on our own. But some are imposed solely for the benefit of others. Some are based on old-fashioned ignorance and take no account of modern knowledge. Yet another category applies only to special situations, such as childhood, but nevertheless carries on into our adult lives.

What would happen if we actually did some of these things? Curiously, most of us admire the rare few who do. And yet we don't dare to be like them ourselves.

Key idea: Make time

Don't convince yourself that there's no time for experimentation or indulgence. How important are all those other things you've just 'got' to do, anyway? Does it matter if the car isn't shiny? Wouldn't letting the grass grow be good for insects and birds? Do the kids really want you to take them to all those after-school activities? Are you certain it's essential to have dinner with those people you don't really like?

Always ask yourself: 'To what extent will this give me the maximum satisfaction of my whole being?'

You'll probably find you have more time than you think.

Let go of your inner child

We're often told to get in touch with our 'inner child'. We all know what it means. It's the idea that our 'inner child' is playful and carefree and that by being childlike once more we can be happy as adults.

However, the reality of childhood is somewhat different. Childhood isn't a free time. On the contrary, it's a straitjacket, or rather the struggle to put you into a straitjacket. As a child you were told you can't do this, you can't do that, you can't do the other. And there are usually good reasons. As a child you lacked the necessary qualities (knowledge, judgement, wisdom, strength, etc.) to deal with certain situations. The problem is that we carry these admonitions into adulthood. No one ever says to us: 'As from today that rule no longer applies.' It's just taken for granted that we'll 'grow up'. But we don't; at least, not completely. At the back of our minds we still harbour those ideas. We still hear the voices of our childhood friends cautioning: 'You're not allowed to do that.'

So get in touch with your inner child. And when you have... let it go. Become an adult. Cut yourself free.

Keep smiling

> Psychoanalysis is much quicker for men than for women. When analysts want to take patients back to childhood, men are already there.

DEALING WITH INHIBITIONS

If you're inhibited by your perception of what other people consider acceptable, bear in mind that other people are inhibited too. If you take your lead from them, you're never going to break free and be yourself. Don't be afraid to set off in a new direction. Indeed, it may well be that if you take the lead, they'll follow you.

Just take it very slowly, one step at a time. It's important to move ahead but, on the other hand, there's no rush. You have a lifetime to deal with your inhibitions and that's often what it takes. But it's great fun.

Case study: Rachel

'We were watching a film together,' says Rachel, 'and it had a pretty sexy scene in it. You couldn't see exactly what was going on but it was something that we'd never done together, although I'd always wanted to. And I looked at my partner and said: "We could do that." And he said: "OK, let's try." And it was great. But it was also kind of sad that I'd never dared to suggest it before.'

Our own life is the instrument with which we experiment with the truth.

Thich Nhat Hanh (b. 1926), Buddhist teacher

Avoiding unhappiness

The flip side of doing what makes you happy is avoiding things that make you unhappy. A lot of Eastern philosophy tends to start with the proposition that that's more or less impossible. That life is full of unavoidable suffering. That the only possible course is to get mentally prepared for it.

But is that really true? Actually, it's not. In the West today, life is very different to, say, the India of 2,500 years ago in the time of the Buddha, when death was an everyday thing. Life then for many people was little other than suffering. But it isn't the case for the majority of people in the West now.

Many of the problems people suffer in the West are avoidable as a lot of suffering is self-inflicted.

In Chapter 2 we saw the impact of negative thinking. In Chapter 3 we saw the impact of negative emotions. There are also negative actions. You're inviting a negative outcome if, for example, you smoke, eat unhealthily, drink too much alcohol or fail to take sufficient exercise.

So many problems we have in our lives are actually brought on by ourselves. Before you do something, ask:

▶ is this likely to make me happy at any time?

▶ is this likely to make me unhappy at some other time?

Key idea: Motivation direction

We're all motivated towards nice things and away from unpleasant things. But, in any given situation, some of us have far more of one type of motivation than the other. Try to work out which kind of motivation works best for you. For example, if you're trying to give up smoking, is it because you want to move away from ill health and expense or is it because you want to move towards more sporting prowess and whiter teeth? Understanding your motivation direction can help you be more effective when making changes to your lifestyle.

Case study: Tim

Tim had gone for a hike along a coastal path in Cornwall in the UK. Although it was February he did something rather surprising. 'I looked down on a little cove,' says Tim, 'and it looked so inviting. I scrambled down, took my boots and socks off and tested the water. It was pretty cold and I was afraid of having a heart attack or something. I was close to giving up on it but I know myself. If I hadn't dared go in I would have been disappointed with myself and miserable for hours. So I stripped off and plunged in. I don't suppose I was in there more than 30 seconds but it was enough. I was so pleased with myself for overcoming my fear I had a stupid grin on my face all the rest of the day.'

But what about problems that are in no way self-induced? If your aim is to be happy should you ignore them, run away from them, give in or fight them? Problems so often stop you being the way you want to be and doing the things you want to do. The aim is to deal with them in such a way that you can continue to be who you are. Here are some do's and don'ts.

▶ Do assess whether or not action is genuinely needed. Quite often situations resolve themselves. If you decide no action is required, then forget about the whole matter.

▶ Do make a clear plan and implement it, if action is needed.

▶ Don't be afraid to retreat. You may decide that the only rational action is to give up on something, to back down, to do something else, to be with someone else, to go somewhere else, etc. That's fine.

▶ Don't, however, hide from a problem. Deciding that no action is needed is not the same thing as hiding. Retreating is not the same thing as hiding. Hiding is just closing your eyes while the problem gets worse and worse. Turning to alcohol, for example, is hiding. It neither removes you from the problem nor makes the problem go away.

▶ Don't dwell on problems. Turning the problem over and over in your mind ten times is like having ten problems rather than just one. Try to think out a solution (there usually is one), of course, but don't keep on telling yourself how terrible the situation is.

▶ Do your best during the daytime and then forget all about it until the next day. Have a 'cut-off' point. Decide that after, say, 9 p.m. you won't deal with problems (unless, of course, it's something that truly requires urgent action). Relax and go to bed saying this to yourself: 'I shall now go to sleep happy in the knowledge that today I tried my best and did everything I could. It's now my responsibility to recharge my batteries. In the morning I'll wake up feeling refreshed and ready to resume action.'

Plan your happy future

Put your stamp on the future as well as on the present. Don't leave it to take care of itself or to others. Ask yourself:

▶ What would I like to be doing in three months' time?

▶ What would I like to be doing in a year's time?

▶ What would I like to be doing in five years' time?

Work out a strategy. Set the wheels in motion. It's important for happiness always to have one project, at the very least, under way and to look forward to it.

When you stand in that sliver of space that is completely and utterly you, then will you be truly awesome, wonderful, magnificent.

Joseph Riggio, lifestyle guru

Breakthrough

Have you discovered what gives you 'the maximum satisfaction of your whole being'?

a Yes, and it's great.

b Yes, but it just isn't practical for me to live that way.

c No.

If you answered 'a' to this, you've made a breakthrough. If you answered 'b', read this chapter again and also review the material on negative thoughts and emotions in Chapters 2 and 3. If you answered 'c' because you haven't yet discovered what causes 'the maximum satisfaction of your whole being', that's perfectly normal. People are very bad at predicting what will make them happy and many such discoveries come about by accident. Read again the section on Running away to happiness – and start running.

Has being more 'you' made you any happier?

a Yes.

b No – I've made changes but I feel just the same.

c I haven't made any changes.

If you answered 'a' to this, you've made a breakthrough. If you answered 'b', are you sure you're being honest with yourself? It's almost impossible that greater self-expression wouldn't result in feeling happier. Perhaps you haven't yet given voice to the 'real you'. Read this chapter again. If you answered 'c' and haven't actually made any changes at all, you also need to reread this chapter. It's rare to reach a state in which no further expansion of self-expression is possible. Take a good look at your life to see where more could be done.

Have you been able to avoid some sources of potential unhappiness?

a Yes.

b No – I'm aware of them but I can't change.

If you answered 'a' to this, you've made a breakthrough. If you answered 'b', then making certain kinds of changes, such as giving up smoking or cutting down on alcohol, can be difficult. And it's true that a great deal of happiness can come from high-risk activities. Is there really any difference between smoking and, say, mountain climbing? Only you can answer that. Many people are willing to risk their health, their lives and their future happiness in, for example, extreme sports. The happiness they get right now outweighs the other considerations. The important thing is to know the risks and to make your own properly informed decision. But there are other kinds of things that don't involve the same kind of balancing act. Do you always put on your seat belt? Do you wear a helmet when horse-riding? Do you tell someone where you're going and what time you expect to be back when you set off on a wilderness hike? These are the kinds of things that have plenty of upside and no downside.

Focus points

The main points to remember from this chapter are:

* there is such a thing as a 'real you' – but there are always things you can do to make changes and improvements
* aim as much as possible for the maximum satisfaction of your whole being
* don't be afraid to run away; it's futile to stay in a situation that is unhappy for everybody – and while you're running you'll discover new things
* variety is vital to happiness – it avoids 'hedonic adaptation'
* avoid things that will make you unhappy.

Keep smiling

'Doctor, I keep thinking I'm a wheelbarrow.'

'Well, you must stop letting people push you around.'

Don't ask yourself what the world needs; ask yourself what makes you come alive. And then go and do that. Because what the world needs is people who have come alive.

Dr Howard Thurman (1900–81),
American author and civil rights leader

Next step

Once you're happy being yourself it becomes much easier to forge happy relationships. People will recognize how genuine you are and they'll warm to you because of that. In Chapter 10, we'll see why relationships are so important for human happiness and what you can do to create and enhance them.

10

Building happy relationships

In this chapter you will learn:

- ► *what our pets can teach us about relationships*
- ► *why relationships are the number one source of happiness*
- ► *why 'projecting' will always end badly*
- ► *why 'acceptance' is the key to happy relationships.*

Of all the means which wisdom acquires to ensure happiness throughout the whole life, by far the most important is friendship.

Epicurus (341–270 BCE), Greek philosopher

God heard us. He sent help. He sent you.

Marianne Williamson (b. 1952), American spiritual activist

To be lonely is an awful thing. In the 19th century, the pioneering French sociologist Emile Durkheim showed that it could even be a death sentence. He discovered that the rate of suicide was higher among the unmarried and divorced than among the married, higher in childless marriages than those with children, higher in urban areas than in villages, higher among loners than among those with plenty of friends.

For social animals, separation means danger. Security comes from being with the family or group. Bad behaviour is punished by being driven out to the periphery of the herd, there to be the most likely target for any predators in the area. Understandably, animals are very anxious to be accepted back within the group as soon as possible. Never forget that you, too, are a social animal.

If you want to predict whether or not people are likely to be happy, you need do little more than assess the quality of their relationships. We depend on relationships as surely as we depend on air. In survey after survey the conclusion is the same. Relationships are the single most important source of human happiness. On average:

▶ people who are married or living with someone are happier than people who live alone

▶ people who are close to their relatives are happier than people who aren't

▶ people who have close friends are happier than people who don't

▶ people who get on well with colleagues are happier than people who experience friction at work

► people who have pets are less stressed, live longer and are happier than those who don't.

Let's see where you are at the moment in terms of relationships.

Self-assessment: How strong are my relationships?

For each of the following groups of statements, choose the one that most closely represents you.

1 I live:

   a with someone to whom I'm very close

   b in a home I share, but not with a partner

   c alone.

2 As regards relatives and friends:

   a I'm very close

   b I'm not very close.

3 At work:

   a I'm good friends with several colleagues

   b I don't have any friends.

4 As regards friends:

   a they know they can count on me and I can count on them

   b we don't get too involved

   c I haven't any.

5 Hugging is:

   a something I do a lot

   b something I prefer to avoid – I'm not a very tactile person.

6 As regards my deepest thoughts and most personal problems:

   a I have someone I can discuss them with

   b I have no one I can discuss them with.

7 As regards people close to me:

   a I feel free to be myself and develop in the way I want

   b I feel they constrain me from being who I am.

8 As regards romance:

   a I'm deeply in love

   b I'm involved with someone but it's not a great passion

   c I'm not in love with anyone.

9 My partner and I are:

   a very supportive of one another

   b very critical of one another

   c I don't have a partner.

10 As regards pets:

   a I get a lot of comfort from mine

   b I'd like some but it's not appropriate at the moment

   c they're too much of a nuisance.

So how did you get on? In all cases, the answer most conducive to happiness is 'a'. That's not to say that if you live alone you can't be happy, or that if you have no pets you can't be happy. But the more things that make a positive contribution to happiness, the happier you're likely to be. Read on to learn more.

Keep smiling

A lonely person goes to see a psychotherapist.

'I have trouble making friends and I'm wondering if you can help – useless as people like you generally are.'

Pets

I'm going to start with pets because it's with our pets that we have the least complicated relationships, and, in a way, the best.

You might think I'm being facetious but I'm not. Just think about it for a moment – the way we love our pets, and the way they love us, is a model for what human relationships should be.

Your love for Fido doesn't depend on him being the most beautiful dog, or the most intelligent, or the most useful, or anything like that. And Fido's love for you doesn't depend on your looks, wealth or the size of your house either. Basically, you love Fido because he loves you. And he loves you because you love him. It's unconditional love.

Stories of the devotion of animals are legion. A terrier that remained for weeks by the body of its dead master in the Lake District in 1805 was commemorated in a painting by Landseer and in a poem by Wordsworth, who recorded:

> Yes, proof was plain that, since the day
>
> When this ill-fated Traveller died,
>
> The Dog had watched about the spot,
>
> Or by his master's side...

Fido's unconditional love does a lot more for you than you may have realized. Hanging out with Fido and, in particular, stroking him:

▶ lowers your blood pressure

▶ reduces your level of the stress hormone cortisol

▶ increases your level of oxytocin, a peptide that makes you feel affectionate as well as increasing the 'happy chemicals' dopamine and serotonin.

Key idea: Pets improve health

In one study, the survival rate for heart-attack patients was 28 per cent higher if there was a pet in the house. The effects are so clear that many hospitals and hospices have animals that visit the patients.

The curious thing is that all of the positive effects can also be achieved through loving, physical contact with other people.

The fact that animals make such a clear difference is proof that we seldom get our human relationships right.

This is all down to expecting too much of the wrong kinds of things from our friends, relatives and partners. And we end up getting less of what we really need. Enjoy people as you enjoy your pet. Don't complicate things. Enjoy them for what they are. And not for what they can do for you.

Pets have other things to teach us, too, such as 'seeing' emotions – which is why your dog disappears the morning before an appointment at the vet or why your horse refuses to be caught when you need to give an injection. When you interact with animals, you have to learn to get rid of your negative emotions – genuinely get rid of them – because animals can read you like a book. That's how they survive.

Key idea: Connecting with nature

A pet, particularly a dog or a horse, is also a doorway back into nature, from which so many of us are now unhappily estranged. I'll have more to say about this in Chapter 12.

Of course, merely buying a pet (or, better still, adopting one from a rescue centre) isn't immediately going to make a profound contribution to your baseline happiness. But as time goes by and you bond, you'll feel the benefits.

Remember this: A pet is for life

Don't forget that animals also have rights and needs. Only get a pet if you're sure you can look after it properly for its whole life.

Here's a joke about the difference between relationships with other humans and dogs – but like all good jokes it has a certain truth about it.

Keep smiling

A dog can be better than a new relationship because:

a dog never wants to know about every other dog you've had

after a year a dog is still pleased to see you

the later you are, the more pleased the dog is

a dog never needs to examine the relationship

a dog never criticizes.

Case study: Doris

Doris was naturally very lonely after her husband died. At 72, she no longer drove and didn't get out much. As the weeks went by she visibly deteriorated mentally and physically. It seemed a care home would be the only solution. In desperation, her daughter Wendy bought her a little white Maltese called Lottie. Almost immediately Doris perked up. She now had a responsibility, a dog to care for and a little companion to show affection to her. She never did go into a care home but lived happily with Lottie until her death at the age of 80.

Try it now: Man's best friend

Even if you have friends enough, and children, relatives and a partner, you should still have a pet. If you're lonely, a pet is essential. What kind of pet is a matter for you. But a pet that lives in the house is going to be a more constant source of all those benefits than one that lives outside. If you don't have any firm ideas, get a dog. Dogs became man's best friend at least 100,000 years ago and are always ready for a good cuddle.

If there's no way you can have a pet, try riding. Horses can be very frightening and intimidating at first, but once you get used to them you can enjoy something you can't get from a dog or cat. You can enjoy being carried, which, for some people, is a very special experience.

Remember this: But don't rush in

Not every dog or cat turns out to be your best friend. There can be personality clashes and some breeds are more difficult to handle than others. Get advice from people who have pets already and don't rush in. Take time over your choice. Where dogs are concerned, professional help with training can be a good idea.

Human relationships

> To eat and drink without a friend is to devour like the lion and the wolf.
>
> Epicurus (341–270 BCE), Greek philosopher

BE TACTILE

We're going to apply the first lesson you've learned from your pet. Count the number of times you stroke your pet in a day. Now resolve that you'll have at least the same amount of physical contact with everyone who's close to you.

We often forget that we too are animals and need to touch and be touched. Why should we have less of this wonderful tonic than a dog does? We cover our bodies completely with clothes most of the time, which already makes it difficult, and, on top of that, we've introduced restrictive social conventions. That we've now become afraid to touch one another is a disaster for happiness.

The amazing substance oxytocin, which increases in your body when you stroke your pet, is vital to your mental health and happiness. But it's no use relying on your dog or cat as your sole source, as oxytocin binds you to whatever you're touching.

In other words, if you want to feel bonded with someone and you want that person to feel bonded with you, touch them. Of course, if someone doesn't want to be touched by you, they're not going to like you because you touch them. Probably the reverse is true! But I'm talking about your partner, your children, your brothers and sisters, your friends and so on – people who do want to be close to you.

Oxytocin's extraordinary role began when you were born. It was responsible for your mother's contractions, it was responsible for making milk flow from her breasts, it was responsible for making her maternal and your father paternal, it made your parents more likely to stick together and it was why they didn't abandon you when you cried for the hundredth time in a day. On top of all that, it helped your brain develop properly – without it some of your brain cells would have died. So if it hadn't been for touch and oxytocin your life would have been very different.

Try it now: Hugging

* If you have a partner, give him or her a hug. Find some place you can put your hand on bare skin.
* If you have children, give them a hug. If they refuse to be hugged, deliver a slap on the back or a squeeze of the shoulders – the very minimum is a high five.
* If you have parents, sisters, brothers, etc., give them all a hug.
* If you have a dog or a cat or any cuddly pet, go and stroke it.
* If there's a tree or some long grass nearby, feel it with your hand.

DON'T PLAY MIND GAMES

Now let's turn to the second lesson you've learned from your pet. Dogs don't play mind games – and nor do other animals. Of course, they like games of the stick-throwing and rolling-about kind. But dogs and animals don't play games of the 'I'll pretend I'm not pleased to see him' kind. They're honest and straightforward.

They're also uninhibited. Inhibition is a special involuntary kind of game-playing and it's one of the great enemies of meaningful relationships and, therefore, of happiness. Inhibitions make us hide part of ourselves away, so we can't fully give ourselves to our friends, relatives and partners. Our inhibitions inhibit others. Our inhibitions make other people think they're seeing reality when they're seeing an illusion. Our inhibitions make liars of us. We pretend we're being honest but we're not.

What we're all seeking is more meaningful contact. We want to engage with other people at a profound level. Talking about the weather hardly constitutes a meaningful engagement. If anything, it's the reverse. It's saying: 'You're not close to me; you're only permitted to talk to me about superficial things.'

So instead of talking about the weather, try talking about things that are more personal and profound – happiness, for example. Or coping with illness or disability. Or dealing with redundancy.

Try it now: Be the first

If you're not intimate with someone, then, by definition, you're separated from that person. If you're not intimate with anybody then you're lonely.

* Don't wait for someone else to be friendly – be the first.
* Don't wait for someone else to introduce an intimate subject – be the first.
* Don't wait for someone else to make a personal disclosure – be the first.
* The more you give, the more you get.

LEARN TO 'SEE' EMOTIONS

The third lesson you can learn from your pet is the visibility of emotions that we discussed above. Of course, you already have a limited ability to 'see' emotions and so does everybody else. But you can develop things much further. If you want to get on well with other people, you have to push your happiness and your love ahead of you so they can easily see it.

You won't be able to push that aura ahead of you if you're a judgemental sort of person. Don't approach others with a feeling of hostility or suspicion, with your positive emotions hidden away behind your back like some precious metal. Other people will sense it.

Key idea: Body language

One way of signalling your empathy with others is by matching their body language. Don't make this too deliberate or obvious, or it will simply come across as artificial and insincere, the opposite of the intended effect. Rather, note when people are, for example, leaning towards you; in that case, you lean forward as well. Or if they're resting their chin on their hand, you might do the same. Done subtly, this works at the subconscious level, making other people feel good about you.

Remember, you can't empathize fully if you're harsh on people who are different from you. For example, if you've never smoked you'll never understand someone who's addicted to nicotine unless you seek to understand it non-judgementally.

Nor, unless you're open-minded, will you be able to relate to people from different social backgrounds, different cultures or different age groups. Obviously, you'll widen your circle of friends if you can understand those differences.

▶ Be interested in other people.

▶ Be compassionate towards other people.

▶ Be responsive – use facial expressions and tone of voice.

▶ Trust people with small things and work up to big things – don't distrust people without reason.

▶ Don't be judgemental.

▶ Try to find something you agree with.

▶ If you disagree, mention the thing you agree with before mentioning the thing you disagree with.

Key idea: Broaden your friendships

If you confine your friendships to people with exactly the same background and outlook as yourself, things will be comfortable and easy. But you'll be limiting your opportunities for growth, new experiences and happiness if you do. And there's one kind of difference most of us are anxious to bridge – the one between the sexes.

Try it now: Expand yourself

Read the passage below about Ernest Hemingway and then try to pump up your aura in the same way.

Something played off him – he was intense, electrokinetic, but in control, a racehorse reined in. He stopped to talk to one of the musicians in fluent Spanish and something about him hit me – enjoyment: God, I thought, how he's enjoying himself! I had never seen anyone with such an aura of fun and well-being. He radiated it and everyone in the place responded.

A. E. Hotchner, writing about his first encounter with the American novelist Ernest Hemingway

LIVING WITH 'THE ONE'

I am in love – and, my God, it is the greatest thing that can happen to a man. I tell you, find a woman you can fall in love with. Do it. Let yourself fall in love. If you have not done so already, you are wasting your life.

D. H. Lawrence (1885–1930), English novelist

Would you be happier if you and your partner separated? It may seem an odd question with which to begin a section on love. But let's get it out of the way now. Because a recent study has shown that when a relationship is unhappy, men and women benefit equally by splitting up. If you're not going to split up, the alternative – the only alternative – is to stay together and make your relationship happy. There is no middle way on this one. Staying together and being unhappy or less than happy is not what you got together for.

It's your right to be happy. And, never forget, it's your partner's, too. So which is it? Are you separating or are you staying together? Make your choice. If you don't have the same goals, if you don't want the same kind of life, if you're not travelling in the same direction, if you stifle one another's creativity rather than enhance it, then you're probably not going to be happy, whatever you do.

Love does not consist in gazing at each other, but in looking outward together in the same direction.

Antoine de Saint-Exupéry (1900–44), French author and pilot

If you've plumped for staying together, read on. You've just committed yourself to building a relationship that makes both of you very happy. And one of the most important ways to do that is to learn something new and wonderful about your partner, yourself and your relationship every day.

One might compare two human beings to two bodies charged with electricity of different potentials. Isolated from each other the electric forces within them are invisible, but if they come into the right juxtaposition the force is transmuted, and a spark, a glow of burning light, arises between them. Such is love.

Marie Stopes (1880–1958), Scottish birth control campaigner

AVOID THE PROJECTION TRAP

Don't copy D. H. Lawrence, whose enthusiastic view of relationships I quoted earlier. Lawrence fell for Frieda Weekley, who became the model and inspiration for many of the female characters in his novels. She left a home, a husband and three young children to be with him. He called her 'the woman of a lifetime'. Before long, he was battering her.

Lawrence made a well-known mistake. He projected onto Frieda the fantasies he wanted to believe in. Remarkable though she was, she was never going to be able to live up to them. Frieda equally projected onto Lawrence her fantasies about great writers. Artistically it was a fruitful combination and it had its heights. But 'happy' is not the word for the relationship.

Happiness comes from discovering a reality much more interesting than anything you could have imagined. If you and your partner have been 'projecting', then at some point you're going to come down to earth with a bump. It's why scientists say that the 'walking on air' feeling just can't last. The most cynical give it just a few weeks. None of them give it more than two years. But they're wrong. And I'll explain how to prove them wrong in a moment.

There's another kind of projection and that's projecting onto the relationship. The composer Wagner provides a pretty good example. This is what he wrote to his fellow composer Liszt: 'As I have never in my life known the real and true joy of love, I will raise a monument to that most beautiful of dreams in which, from beginning to end, this love is truly and entirely fulfilled.' The monument was his most passionate opera in which Isolde literally dies of love on the corpse of Tristan.

It's a beautiful vision in a way. Rather unromantically, psychologists call it the 'collapse of ego boundaries'. The two had become one in life. And in Wagner's extreme fantasy they also had to be one in death. But having a woman dying of love on a daily basis doesn't get the kids bathed. Wagner wouldn't have known true love if he was staring it in the face because he was looking for the wrong signs. His problem was that he didn't realize that getting the shopping was love. He was too caught up in a world of myths and make-believe, as well as his own megalomania.

Love, and you shall be loved.

Ralph Waldo Emerson (1803–82),
American philosopher and poet

RULES FOR WALKING ON AIR

That 'walking on air' feeling comes from the chemical PEA, of which we get a huge hit in the early days of a relationship. You never achieve quite the same levels later in a relationship, even using the additional techniques we've discussed in the chapters on eating and exercise, because there's an element that comes with novelty. But you can stay high all your life if you follow these rules.

▶ **Four kinds of acceptance**

Rule number 1. Accept your partner's love. You don't, like Wagner, insist it has to be expressed in a particular way. You have to be free to express your love your way and your partner has to be free to do the same. Simply enjoy the love. Bathe in it. Be grateful for it, because it's a wonderful thing.

Rule number 2. Accept the way your partner is. You don't, like D. H. Lawrence, tell your partner how to dress or behave or what to think or anything else. In other words, you don't project your fantasies onto your partner.

Rule number 3. Accept your partner's growth. You don't try to keep your partner the way he/she was at the beginning of the relationship. You both have to be free to develop. In fact, learn to love change. Because if there were no change, there could be no improvement. Would you really want your partner to be the same at the age of, say, 40 as when you first met 20 years earlier? Not to know any more? Not to have acquired any more skills? Not to have more insight and wisdom?

Rule number 4. Accept that two people are different and always will be (especially if one is a man and the other a woman). You already love some of the differences. Learn to love all of them.

Try it now: Relish the differences

Draw a line down the middle of some sheets of paper from top to bottom. On the left, make a list of all the differences you have with your partner. On the right, set out all the things that are puzzling about those differences but also all the things that are wondrous about them. Have your partner do the same. Then discuss what you've written.

Remember this: Love the real person

Acceptance isn't about getting together with the first person who comes along. That's not what it means. Acceptance means being in love with the way a person really is, not with the way you'd like that person to be.

▶ Nine further rules

Rule number 5. Always remain curious. Your partner is actually an inexhaustible mine. You'll never run out of treasures as long as you keep digging new galleries.

Rule number 6. Always give support. Support is very important for both sexes but especially for women, who have a strong need to be able to talk about themselves and their problems. In one study, 41 per cent of women who suffered a 'stressful life event' became depressed if they were given only a low level of support by their partners, but the figure fell to 10 per cent with a high level of support. Another study found that relationships in which partners react enthusiastically to one another's good news are the happiest; don't be grudging or uninterested.

Rule number 7. Always build your partner up. We've already seen how damaging negative thoughts and emotions can be. If you foster them in your partner – possibly as a way of gaining dominance in the relationship – you'll end up destroying him or her. Don't criticize and, above all, never make personal attacks.

Rule number 8. Talk, talk, talk – and make it meaningful. One study found that talking to a woman is more meaningful than talking to a man. Both men and women reported that talking to a woman resulted in a conversation that was pleasanter, more intimate and – this is very important – with more self-disclosure. If you're a man, learn to be meaningful.

Rule number 9. Don't make comparisons (see Chapter 2). Don't say or even think: 'he/she earns more money than my partner'.

Rule number 10. Don't hold onto negative thoughts or emotions (see Chapters 2 and 3).

Rule number 11. Provide plenty of physical contact. As we saw earlier, oxytocin is essential to your health as well as to the health of your relationship.

Rule number 12. Have plenty of sex. Sex is the source of several 'happy chemicals'. One study found that satisfaction with a relationship correlates very closely with frequency of intercourse minus the number of rows.

Rule number 13. Do something happy together every day.

Case study: Yvonne

Yvonne had grown up in a household where there had been a lot of shouting. So when she married Oliver it was almost inevitable she'd carry on in the same way. As far as she was concerned she was 'clearing the air'. And it could get pretty vicious. Every time there was a disagreement the insults flew – and Oliver responded by withdrawing. Within two years the marriage was on the rocks and the couple went for counselling. Yvonne was taught a very different way of dealing with disagreements – calmly and without making personal criticisms. Unfortunately, it took the shock of divorce to drive the message home. Yvonne now lives with a new partner and is careful not to shout or make personal attacks. 'I didn't realize,' she says, 'the damage I was doing.'

Breakthrough

Have you been able to improve any relationships and, if so, have they in turn increased your happiness?

a Yes.

b No, relationships are just the same.

c No, I'm all alone, though I don't want to be.

If you answered 'a', you're ready to move on to the next chapter. If you answered 'b', read through this chapter again and try following all the 13 rules to see what develops. It's also worth looking again at Chapter 2. Some of the negative styles of thinking described there are as relevant to relationships as to other kinds of situations. Are you comparing, for example? (His wife is more fun.) Are you demanding more and more? (He just doesn't show as much affection as I need.) Are you insisting on perfection? (Why can't he dress more stylishly?) Are you using labels? (Mean Uncle Bert.) If you answered 'c', then for the moment you have to cultivate other sources of happiness. That's a useful skill, because we're all going to find ourselves alone at some time. Try to look at this period as a positive learning opportunity. It need not last long. There's a world full of people actively looking for friendship and love just as you are. You might also like to read *Teach Yourself Confidence and Social Skills*.

Focus points

The main points to remember from this chapter are:

* relationships are the single most important source of human happiness
* if you're lonely, consider getting a pet; if you're not lonely, still consider getting a pet – stroking a pet reduces stress and improves health
* love people the way you love your pet – unconditionally
* oxytocin binds you to other people – the more touching, the more bonding
* resolve to make your relationship happy – there's no middle way between that and separation.

Keep smiling

The teacher puts a sentence on the blackboard and asks the class to punctuate it correctly.

The boys do it like this: 'Woman, without her man, is nothing.'

The girls do it like this: 'Woman: without her, man is nothing.'

Next step

When you have a romantic relationship you have sex. But sex can be much more than a discharge of sexual tension. In Chapter 11, we'll see how sex can be an important factor in spiritual experience, personal growth, bonding, fun and happiness.

11

A happy sex life

In this chapter you will learn:

- ▶ *why sex is the most important activity for happiness*
- ▶ *why getting rid of inhibitions is essential for happy sex*
- ▶ *how chemicals released during sex make us happy*
- ▶ *which techniques produce the maximum happiness.*

> Praise be to God who has placed the source of man's greatest pleasure in woman's natural parts, and woman's greatest pleasure in the natural parts of man!
>
> *The Perfumed Garden*, a 15th-century
> Arabic work of erotic literature

If you have a partner, sex is the most wonderful thing you can do together to create happiness. Some people talk of 'just sex'. If this includes you, then you can't yet have experienced sex to the full, which means you have something marvellous to look forward to.

Never think in terms of 'just sex'. It would be like saying 'just love' or describing the Milky Way as 'just a load of gas' or Rodin's sculptures as 'just a pile of minerals'. 'Just sex' exists but that's not what we're concerned with here. We're talking about sex as the thrilling, endlessly fascinating and incredibly beautiful way two souls unite and, in uniting, discover they're also united with the whole universe, which is going to make you feel very happy indeed.

Let's see how happy a sex life you're having.

Self-assessment: How happy is my sex life?

For each of the ten following questions choose the answer that most represents you.

1 Sex with my partner is:

   a one of the top five sources of happiness

   b a minor source of happiness

   c a source more of conflict than happiness.

2 My partner and I:

   a cuddle a lot – skin contact is very important to us

   b cuddle a bit before and after sex, but that's about it

   c cuddle only rarely.

3 My partner and I:

    a have sex regularly

    b wait until we're overcome by lust – then we have sex

    c have very different sex drives.

4 My partner and I:

    a make sex a priority

    b don't have much time for sex – there are so many things to do.

5 My partner and I:

    a often spend an hour or more having sex with music, candles and incense.

    b usually have quickies – it's all over in ten minutes.

6 My partner and I:

    a tell one another what we want in bed

    b are both too inhibited to say what we want in bed.

7 My partner and I:

    a are always trying new things in bed

    b stick to the things we know we like in bed.

8 My partner and I:

    a tell one another our sexual fantasies

    b would never dare swap sexual fantasies.

9 I think sex:

    a isn't just a physical thing; it's also very important emotionally and spiritually.

    b is just a physical thing.

10 In our relationship:

    a we're faithful to one another

    b one of us has had an affair

    c both of us have had affairs.

I'm not just speaking for myself in stressing the importance of sex; my view is supported by scientists and statisticians. In 2003, five researchers asked 1,000 *women* to rate 19 activities in terms of the happiness they produced. Sex was rated the activity that produces the single largest amount of happiness.

I've italicized 'women' to emphasize that it's not only men, as some would have us believe, who think that sex produces happiness. (And if you want to know what came bottom of the list, it was commuting to and from work.)

The point is reinforced by Andrew Oswald, Professor of Economics at Warwick University in the UK and David Blanchflower of Dartmouth College in the USA. They analysed data on 16,000 adult Americans and concluded: 'There is little evidence… that men enjoy sex slightly more than women.' This is a rather lukewarm way of saying that sex makes men and women equally happy.

Oswald and Blanchflower's next conclusion is even more important. They didn't pin down exactly the optimum amount but observed that: 'Having sex at least four times a week is associated with approximately 0.12 happiness points.' These 'happiness points' are highly significant. In clearer language the researchers had this to say: 'The more sex, the happier the person.'

Very significantly they also noted that: 'Celibacy and small amounts of sex have statistically indistinguishable effects upon happiness.' In other words, a lot of sex produces a lot of happiness but a little sex produces almost none.

It seems, however, that very few people actually know what makes them happy (see Chapter 9) because only around 7 per cent of Americans reported having sex four times a week or more.

Key idea: Sex and the older man

If you're not having sex very often and if it's because you're a mature man who finds it physically difficult to have sex several times a week, help is at hand. As you'll see below, there is a technique that will allow most older men to do just that.

Let's turn from the scientists to the poets. Shelley defined love as 'the universal thirst for a communion not merely of the senses, but of our whole nature, intellectual, imaginative and sensitive…'. He then went on to define the role of sex in the following terms: 'The sexual impulse, which is only one, and often a small part of those claims, serves, from its obvious and external nature, as a kind of expression of the rest.'

In other words, sex can be communion on every level: total union; the end of separation; a oneness; the end of loneliness; happiness.

The elements of happy sex

The kind of sex that I'm talking about has several elements, of which the most important are:

▶ love

▶ monogamy

▶ absence of guilt

▶ absence of inhibition

▶ spirituality

▶ frequency.

LOVE AND MONOGAMY

Most people can enjoy sex without being in love. And sex between freely consenting adults who are not in love is, for many people, far better than no sex at all. But the optimum sex, the kind of sex I want to deal with here, can only be achieved by two people who love one another.

The scientists back me up on this. Oswald and Blanchflower found that, in the course of a year, the number of sexual partners for maximum happiness is one. That's right – one. (And if they'd asked not about the past year but the past 5 or 10 or 20 years they would have got the same result.) People who had sex outside of their marriage had low happiness scores, and so did those who had ever paid for sex. So, there's no need to feel envious of rock stars who report having had sex with hundreds or even thousands of partners. It may or may not thrill a particular individual to behave like that, but for most people it's not the way to happiness.

Remember this: The pleasure of monogamy

We don't have to look very far for an explanation of the pleasures of monogamy. Ultimate sex, as Shelley observed, involves communion on every level. But if you're not in love, you won't be fully open to your partner on any of those levels, not even the purely physical.

ABSENCE OF GUILT

We talked about guilt and the need to get rid of it in Chapters 2 and 3. So let's see how you're getting on. Can you say you feel no guilt about your sexual practices or fantasies? Probably not – because no subject is the cause of so much guilt as sex. And that's a great pity, because sex is potentially an immense source of happiness. Guilt spoils it. One of the most important things you can do, therefore, in your search for greater happiness, is to overcome those guilty feelings.

It's extraordinary that, between healthy consenting adults, something so harmless, something that creates so much pleasure, should be the subject of so many interdictions. Astonishing, too, that so many people should be so concerned about, indeed terrified of, what other people are doing in the privacy of their own bedrooms. As recently as 2009 the Supreme Court of Alabama actually outlawed the sale of any device 'primarily for the stimulation of human genital organs'.

In the USA in 1994, Joycelyn Elders was fired as Surgeon General by President Clinton for putting forward the eminently sensible idea that masturbation, as an alternative to intercourse, could help in the fight against AIDS. And several states of the USA still have laws against oral sex. Given this kind of propaganda it's not surprising there should be so much guilt surrounding the subject.

Let me ask you a few questions. Would you say your thyroid gland was immoral? Would you say your right lung was evil? Would you say your left kidney was naughty? Absurd, right? Yet that's the way we tend to think of testicles and vaginas and all the rest of those bits 'down there'.

Even scientists allow their objectivity to be clouded by their fear of pleasure. The psychiatrist Viktor Frankl, whom we met in Chapter 9, wrote in his book *Man's Search For Meaning*:

> 'The more a man tries to demonstrate his sexual potency or a woman her ability to experience orgasm, the less they are able to succeed. Pleasure is, and must remain, a side effect or by-product, and is destroyed and spoiled to the degree to which it is made a goal in itself.'

This, of course, is complete rubbish. The record for male ejaculations is believed to be 16 in an hour while for female orgasms it's believed to be 134. And they didn't happen by accident. They happened as a result of people *trying*. The only reason pleasure is 'spoiled' by its pursuit is if you feel guilty about enjoying yourself.

So how can you stop feeling guilty about sex?

The bad news is that it's not something that can be done in a day. Those guilty feelings were probably created over a period of years and they'll take a long time to eradicate. The good news is that working on them is both a fascinating journey and a lot of fun.

Try it now: Getting rid of sex guilt

Here are a few ideas to help:

* Read some sex manuals. (You might like to start with *Have Great Sex* and *Get Intimate With Tantric Sex*, both written by me and available in the Teach Yourself series.)
* Read some sex surveys. There's no reason, of course, that you should copy other people but you may find it reassuring to know what other people do in bed. You'll find plenty online.
* Watch an erotic film together.
* Discuss the things you'd like to do (books and films can be good ways of starting the conversation). You may be afraid your partner will think you weird but, in all probability, he or she is probably just as afraid of being thought weird by you.
* Go to a sex shop with your partner, or visit an online sex shop together, buy something and try it out.
* Use self-hypnosis to deal with 'hang-ups' (see Chapter 6). 'See' yourself starting to explore the thing that bothers you. In subsequent sessions 'see' yourself going further and further. Repeat the visualization over several days until you feel quite comfortable using the sex technique in real life.
* Have sex frequently. Every day if possible. The more often you have sex the more normal it will seem and the less guilty you will feel.

ABSENCE OF INHIBITION

We've already talked about inhibition in the context of 'being yourself' (Chapter 9). It's especially important when it comes to sex. The fact that you're in love doesn't by any means guarantee that your sex life, or any other part of your life together, will be uninhibited. But unless you're uninhibited, communion on every level can't take place.

Even nowadays, despite all the media exposure to sexual images and all the talk of sexual liberation, many people are still frightened of sex. If you feel the need to drink alcohol in order to have sex, this includes you.

It's very rare for parents to talk about sex in a positive way. In fact, it's rare for anybody to talk about sex in a positive way. Even sex educators tend to concentrate on the perils of sex rather than its pleasures. So it's no surprise that it can take years or even decades to overcome our inhibitions (meanwhile, perhaps, passing them on to the next generation).

SPIRITUALITY

Sex won't be fully rewarding unless it involves a spiritual element. That's to say, communion on far more than a purely physical level. When spirituality enters the picture, you feel that you're making contact with the secret essence of your partner, that the physical boundary between you and your partner no longer exists, nor that between the two of you and the rest of the universe.

Using sexual energy for spirituality is known as tantric sex. It's dealt with in more detail below.

> The more sensitive, the more romantic, and the more idealistic is the young person of either sex, the more his or her soul craves for some kindred soul with whom the whole being can unite.
>
> Marie Stopes (1880–1958),
> Scottish birth control campaigner

FREQUENCY

Most couples don't have sex often enough to enjoy the full benefits. According to Oswald and Blanchflower, couples should cuddle naked every day and aim for intercourse at least four times a week.

Case study: Pat and David

How often to have sex is a frequent source of friction. That's certainly what Pat and David found. Pat thought she wanted sex about once a week on a Sunday afternoon and was irritated by David's attempts to get her into bed more often. Then one day they had sex before getting up. 'I feel too tired at night,' says Pat, 'but in the morning I really enjoyed it. So we did it again the next day. And the next. I was really surprised at myself.' Pat estimates they now have sex four or five mornings a week.

Keep smiling

> A psychologist gives a man an ink blot test. The client
> studies the first blot and announces, 'That's a man and a
> woman having sex.' The psychologist then produces two
> more blots and the client gives the same reply. 'It's clear
> you're obsessed with sex,' says the psychologist. 'Me!'
> exclaims the client. 'You're the one who keeps showing me
> dirty pictures.'

How does sex make you happy?

However ecstatic sex may make you feel at the time, can it
fundamentally alter your level of happiness the other, shall
we say, 163 hours of the week? The answer is that, yes, sex
can make you feel happy both at the time and for a while
afterwards. One of the reasons is that sex increases the level of
certain 'happy' chemicals in the body. Do it often enough and
the effect will never leave you.

► **dopamine** – this is the neurotransmitter that makes sex and
  everything else that's pleasurable, pleasurable. Without
  it, you wouldn't have the motivation to get out of bed in
  the morning. With it, you can't wait to get back into bed.
  Dopamine increases sex and sex increases dopamine. It's
  what makes you feel ecstasy and rapture. A beneficial side-
  effect is that when your dopamine is high from sex you won't
  be so interested in drugs or alcohol.

► **phenylethylamine** (**PEA**) – this is the chemical that produces
  that 'walking on air' feeling. It's an amphetamine-like substance
  that stimulates dopamine and is naturally high in the early days
  of a love affair. If you want to keep it high throughout your
  relationship, have plenty of sex, because it peaks at orgasm.

► **oxytocin** – when you enjoy oxytocin together with someone
  else you're bonded. You're far more likely to stay together
  and you're far more likely to forget previous partners. If you
  want your relationship to endure, you want oxytocin. And
  how do you get it? By touching and particularly by having
  plenty of sex because it also peaks at orgasm. Like PEA,
  oxytocin increases dopamine too.

You can see that these three chemicals together can create an extremely potent 'happy' cocktail. There's one other vital element: semen makes women happy. At first, it may sound ridiculous. But there's good scientific evidence for it. And even before there was scientific evidence, sexual philosophers have believed it for hundreds and even thousands of years. In fact, the mingling of male and female 'essences' is fundamental to the Chinese philosophy of Taoism. If you've heard of yin and yang, you've already got an understanding of it. Yin is the female principle and yang is the male principle. The two have to be in harmony in both men and women, as well as throughout the universe.

In Taoist thought, that harmony can be brought about during sex, when not only can a woman absorb a man's yang essences (now proven) but a man can absorb a woman's yin essences (not proven, to my knowledge). It's fascinating to reflect that the Taoists already held these beliefs more than two millennia ago. In the West these beliefs are more recent but they have a pedigree. Marie Stopes, whose name endures through the clinics she set up, wrote the same in her ground-breaking book *Married Love*, published in 1918.

So what is this proof? A team led by Gordon Gallup, a psychologist at the State University of New York, looked for a relationship between the sex lives of women and their degree of happiness, using the Beck Depression Inventory (a standard questionnaire for assessing mood). The team discovered that women whose partners never used condoms were significantly happier than women whose partners always or usually used condoms. The unhappiest were the women who weren't having any sex at all.

After controlling for various factors, Gallup and his team concluded that the happiest women were, indeed, absorbing 'happy' chemicals from their partners' semen through the wall of their vagina. This is not so surprising, in fact, because semen contains mood-altering hormones including testosterone, oestrogen, follicle-stimulating hormone, luteinizing hormone, prolactin and several prostaglandins. Some of these chemicals from a partner's semen have been detected in women's bloodstreams soon after sex.

Remember this: Condoms

Sexually transmitted diseases and unwanted pregnancies would more than offset any of the psychological benefits of semen. If you need to use condoms, you should continue to do so.

How to have happy sex

You now know about some of the 'sex chemicals' involved in happiness. How can you have sex so as to optimize those chemicals and, therefore, happiness?

▶ Rule number 1: lots of cuddling

As we've seen, oxytocin is a very desirable chemical. The way to optimize it is to touch as often and as completely as possible. Sleep naked and start every day with a naked cuddle. Use every opportunity you can. Cuddling shouldn't only be a prelude to sex. It's important in its own right.

Try it now: Cuddling positions

* Spooning. A lovely position to adopt when you're naked in bed together, drifting off to sleep or slowly waking up. You lay on your sides, facing the same way, nicely relaxed and pressed together.
* Whole body embrace. This is the best way of maximizing contact. You lay one on top of the other, face to face. Your feet should touch.
* The armchair. A great position when you both want to read or watch television. One of you sits on the floor or bed, legs apart, to make a kind of armchair, and the other sits between the legs, facing the same direction.
* The sitting embrace. When you want to talk, or share a drink, or feed one another appetizers, this is how you do it. One of you sits on the floor or bed cross-legged and the other sits on the first one's lap, so you're face to face.

▶ Rule number 2: self-expression

In Chapter 9 we looked at the importance of self-expression. This applies as much to sex as to everything else. If you're afraid of the consequences of your own self-expression, or your partner's, don't be. Self-expression is liberating and your relationship will be all the better for it. You'll be happier.

As regards sexual techniques, there are bound to be things you'd like to do sexually that you and your partner haven't done before. This can be delicate. Of course, when passion takes over, it's normal to explore new territory without consciously thinking about it and your partner may equally be carried along. It could be your partner wants to try these things as well and has been waiting for you to take the lead. But it isn't fair to try to do something you know your partner isn't happy with. Discussion and compromise are the ways forward.

Fantasies can be a problem area. We all have sexual fantasies. The question is how much you should tell your partner. Ideally you should be able to reveal all your sexual fantasies and your partner should be able to do likewise. After all, your fantasies, sexual or otherwise, are part of your personality. If you feel you have to hide your fantasies from your partner, you're not free and you can't be fully happy.

One of the fears is that fantasies reflect genuine desires. Relax. Most sexual fantasies couldn't come true anyway. They tend to involve people with perfect bodies who behave exactly as the fantasist wants. They don't have any sexually transmitted diseases or body odour. They're never jealous or shy or inhibited and so on.

On the other hand, you might fantasize about things that are perfectly possible and you might go on to try them, if that's what you both want.

Generally speaking, the least threatening and most common fantasies are those that only involve the two of you exploring new techniques or places to make love. Going a little further, some people are excited by the idea of an audience. Typical examples are being on display, being filmed naked or people watching while you make love.

Remember this: Be cautious

Couldn't fantasies be a source of unhappiness rather than happiness? Of course they could. As I said at the beginning, sharing fantasies is an ideal but it's one you might not be able to fully attain.

Try it now: Expanding your repertoire

* Express your artistic side. Take turns to choose the ambience, so you both get the chance to express your personalities. Flowers, perfumes, incense, music (see below), the colour and material of the sheets, mood lighting, candles... Why not go even further? Say, a four-poster bed, mirrors, Arabian-style drapes as if you're in a tent in the desert, sound effects, a striptease dance...

* Get rid of inhibitions. It's important to make a conscious decision to fight inhibition. The journey can be a long one but it's extremely interesting. And every step forward brings a reward. Buy a sex manual (there are suggestions at the end of this book) and both read it. Make a list of the things you'd like to try. Then agree you'll set aside, say, one session a month for experimentation. That way, neither of you is under any pressure on the other occasions. There's no need to be in a rush. Don't be despondent if your partner is more inhibited than you are. On the other hand, don't be defensive if your partner is more adventurous than you are. Just take things slowly, one step at a time. If one of you tries to hurry things, the other may get frightened, which would be a shame. If you're the inhibited one, try using visualization during meditation (Chapter 7) to get used to new ideas.

* Fantasies. If you want to tease out your partner's fantasies, and reveal your own, just hint at something when you're having sex and see what your partner's reaction is. If your partner tenses up and doesn't respond, you may well be on the wrong track. It certainly doesn't mean your partner isn't interested in any sexual fantasies at all. Maybe you just got the wrong one. Don't press it for now. Try something else a few days later.

▶ **Rule number 3: music**

Dr Johnson called music the only sensual pleasure without vice. Shakespeare called it the food of love. If it's fast and furious, sex is fast and furious. If it's languid, sex is languid. Music has a powerful effect on us even if we're not consciously aware of it.

Without any doubt, music is the most mysterious of the arts, working in ways that still aren't fully understood. But we know that when a piece of music gives you 'that funny feeling', it's stimulating the reward structures of the brain. Music can go as directly to your brain as a recreational drug, and some cultures have deplored it for that very reason. At the same time, activity in the amygdala is inhibited. That's the part of the brain associated with fear. So music can make you feel confident – always a good thing where sex is concerned – and augment arousal. It's indispensable.

If you want proof, scientists have found that music we like tends to:

▶ lower cortisol, the stress hormone

▶ lower testosterone, a hormone that can cause irritability and aggression

▶ increase oxytocin, the 'touch' hormone

▶ increase endorphins, the body's painkillers.

Lower cortisol reduces anxiety, including performance anxiety, which is a good thing before sex. Lower testosterone may sound like a bad thing where sex is concerned. But testosterone seems more related to desire than function and, since you've already got the desire when you put the music on, there shouldn't be a problem. However, it seems that some music may increase testosterone – if you feel the need for more testosterone, go for something a little more aggressive. Higher oxytocin will increase skin sensation, including around the genitals. It also increases dopamine and serotonin. Throw in increased endorphins and you've the ingredients for a big high.

Try it now: Experiment with music

Select several quite different pieces of music. Play each of them for a few minutes as you make love. How did they influence what you did and what you felt?

▶ Rule number 4: multiple orgasms for women

Years ago women didn't have orgasms because they didn't expect to have orgasms (nor did their partners expect them to). Now, the majority of women have one orgasm because they expect to have just one orgasm. Some of them are completely satisfied by their single orgasm, and that's fine. But the more orgasms you have, then (within reason) the more of those 'happy chemicals' you'll enjoy.

The way to unlock your multi-orgasmic capacity is not through intercourse but through masturbation. Have your one orgasm by your usual solo method. But don't have it in the back of your mind that you'll settle for one. Be optimistic. Now simply continue to play with your clitoris. It may well be that you'll surprise yourself by having a second orgasm without doing anything different, and a third. If not, you're going to have to do something unusual, something extra, to get those additional orgasms.

Try it now: Getting those orgasms

* Put on some sensual, very rhythmical music.
* Strip completely naked, if you're not already.
* Relax. Give yourself an hour to succeed.
* Rub yourself all over with some body oil.
* Stimulate other places in addition to your clitoris – the entrance to your vagina, your G-spot area, your anus, your nipples... whatever excites you.
* Use a vibrator.
* Try watching an erotic video or DVD or yourself in a mirror.
* Increase the blood flow by spanking yourself.
* Try different positions. On your back, open your legs as far as you can or, alternatively, press them hard together with the vibrator between your thighs and against your vulva. Or try kneeling with your thighs open and lean back as far as you can – use some pillows to support you. The more physical tension you create the better.
* Use fantasy.
* Speak your fantasy out loud.
* Focus.
* Make plenty of noise.

▶ Rule number 5: simultaneous orgasms

Simultaneous orgasms as the apogee of great sex go in and out of fashion. But where happy sex is concerned they're always a good idea. The ideal is for a woman to have several orgasms before the man has his and then to have one 'big one' together. This brings the active stage of lovemaking to an end and you can then both fully luxuriate in that wonderful glow.

Try it now: Coordinating climaxes

The key is in being able to influence your own and your partner's sexual excitement so that, together, you can get coordinated.

* Words: simply tell your partner what stage you're at. Then your partner has the chance to speed up or slow down. You can also use sounds and 'talking dirty' to increase excitement.
* Buttons: we all have 'buttons' our partners can press or which we can press ourselves to increase excitement. The clitoris is the obvious 'button' for a woman but there are others. For a man, a finger on the anus can often be enough. Have fun discovering your own and one another's 'buttons'.

Key idea: Men don't have to ejaculate

Although most couples find simultaneous orgasms hugely satisfying, there is a technique that comes under the heading of tantric sex by which the man does not ejaculate. Nevertheless, the woman can enjoy multiple orgasms and the man a whole series of 'mini-orgasms', leaving both of you very happy indeed. The technique is explained below.

▶ Rule number 6: avoiding the sexual hangover – multiple orgasms for men

So far I've talked of sex unreservedly as a generator of happiness. But the chemical changes in the body following sex can sometimes send you down rather than up. This happens to men far more than to women, and to older men far more than to younger men. It comes about most of all when men ejaculate too much, as excess ejaculation leads to depletion of serotonin.

Serotonin, you may remember, is a chemical that helps make us feel contented. Other chemicals are involved as well, but if we don't have enough serotonin we're liable to feel anxious and aggressive. It's this that's known as the sexual hangover and, apart from anything else, it can spoil the post-sex period for hours or even days.

From the point of view of sexual hangover, how much ejaculation is too much? A simple test is this: do you feel glowing, elated and happy after ejaculation or slightly lower than you were before? If it's the latter, you're ejaculating too often.

Remember this: The older you are the fewer the ejaculations

Every man is different but as a rough guide think in terms of three to five ejaculations a week in youth, one to three a week in middle age, and one to two a month in old age.

But there seems to be a paradox here. How can you have sex frequently enough to make both of you happy, but without the man ejaculating so often that he gets a hangover? The solution is simple. Some of the time the man has sex without ejaculating.

It's this that's known as 'multiple orgasms for men'. If you're puzzled by this, it may be because you think orgasm and ejaculation are the same thing, but they are not. The word 'ejaculation' covers the emission of fluid. The word 'orgasm' covers the highly pleasurable muscular contractions. Normally the two go together. But you can learn to orgasm without ejaculating.

Having multiple orgasms doesn't mean having several of the kind of orgasm you have now. They are totally different.

▶ The first of a series of multiple orgasms is not as powerful as a conventional orgasm and ejaculation but the combined effect of all the orgasms in a series far exceeds normal experience.

▶ You won't suffer the sexual hangover.

▶ You can prolong lovemaking.

- You won't lose your sexual vitality in the way you do with 'ordinary' sex.

- You and your partner can have sex more often – once a day, for example, or even several times a day.

- Your hormone balance will be different – you'll feel more affectionate and loving.

- You'll feel 'mystical'.

- You'll never be afraid of not being able to perform.

Key idea: Great sex is in the brain

It's in the brain that multiple orgasms are so exquisite. Once you get good at the technique, you'll find that each is more powerful than the previous one. Eventually you'll reach a state of ecstasy.

So how can you experience these multiple orgasms?

Different sexologists describe different methods. One involves strengthening a muscle known as the PC muscle until it can shut off the ejaculation. Another involves pressing a special point (the 'million dollar point') between the testicles and the anus. And there are others.

I'm not going to describe any of these physical techniques. Some require months of training, some interfere too much with lovemaking, some are painful and some don't work. Instead, here is a simple technique that requires nothing other than the power of your mind, which is considerable.

Try it now: Controlling ejaculation

The first step is to practise the technique during masturbation. You probably already use stop/go as a way of prolonging your pleasure. That simply means that you stop stimulating yourself once you get 'too' excited, let your erection subside a little, then begin again. For multiple orgasms, you simply have to refine that technique so you can get closer and closer to the point of no return without 'going over the edge' into ejaculation.

In order to experience orgasm without ejaculation, you have to get very, very close to this point. At the critical moment you have to cease physical and mental stimulation instantly:

❋ stop stroking your penis.

❋ stop thrusting movements.

❋ stop all muscle tension (for example, lower your legs if they're in the air).

❋ stop breathing or, alternatively, pant (experiment to see what works best for you).

❋ stop fantasizing (if you were).

❋ stop looking at sexy images (if you were).

❋ stop 'talking dirty' (if you were).

❋ stop concentrating on the sensations.

In other words, you have to turn off like a light. Once you've achieved multiple orgasms solo, you can start employing the technique with your partner.

Key idea: Partial orgasms build on one another

Don't be surprised if you don't experience much excitement from your first partial orgasm. It doesn't mean you've done anything 'wrong'. The second will be better, and the third better still. Eventually, you'll experience sensations that'll be almost unbearably exquisite.

Remember this: Happy chemicals

Your partner won't be denied 'happy chemicals' altogether if you withhold ejaculation because a certain amount of fluid always leaks from the penis during multiple orgasms. It just won't be as much. On the other hand, you'll be able to have sex more often.

▶ **Rule number 7: tantric (or sacred) sex**

This is the most important rule and now that you've mastered the previous six you're ready for it. The pop star Sting became famous for his five-hour tantric sex sessions. But tantric sex is not primarily about numbers of hours. It's about using sexual energy for spiritual purposes. You may not want to have this style of sex every time, but when you do, it will take you to a higher plane of happiness.

Nobody knows for sure how or when tantra arose but it was probably in India more than 2,000 years ago. It ties in with Hindu beliefs about the origin of the visible universe as described in the Vedas, which is that at one time there was neither what is, nor what is not. In the infinite peace the ONE was breathing. The ONE is pictured as a male god and given the name Shiva. Shiva was lonely and so created Shakti, the female. At that moment, the visible universe came into being, composed of opposites, male and female, positive and negative, matter and anti-matter, and so on.

Sex was just one aspect of tantra, not the whole of it as many people think. It was – and is – the reuniting of the male and female so as to experience the Divine Consciousness. The sensations of sex were believed to be a foretaste of the infinite joy that would be experienced by those who eventually escaped 'the cycle of death and rebirth'.

Recently, tantric sex has been adopted in the West and changed out of all recognition. Almost anything that has to do with a more gentle, considerate, imaginative – and lengthy – style of sex is now given the tantric tag. But this misses the point. Tantric sex is not about particular techniques but about spirituality. If a spiritual experience is the aim, the tantric tag is valid. Anything else is, well, not tantra.

Case study: Ben

Ben read about tantric sex and non-ejaculation in an earlier edition of this book and decided to give it a go. 'I'll never forget the first time,' he says. 'For the rest of the day I was just ambling about, singing to myself, talking to flowers and all that sort of thing. After a long session of non-ejaculatory sex I'm in a state of bliss. Of course I ejaculate sometimes – about once a week – but I would never go back to the old way of having sex.'

Only when souls flowing together, acting as one, distinct in individuality, but united in their action are thus mated, are the psycho-physiological laws met and satisfied.

Alice Bunker Stockham (1833–1912),
American gynaecologist

Key idea: Tantra and tradition

Traditional tantric practices included such bizarre things as public sex with strangers and sex on graves. But we're concerned with happiness and so the modern adaptation I would make is to exclude those kinds of things. For happiness, tantric sex should be confined to a loving, monogamous relationship.

So how do you go about building the spiritual element?

Try it now: Becoming Shiva and Shakti

The first step is to recognize your partner as a manifestation of the Divine Consciousness – one of you is Shiva and the other Shakti. If that sounds too religious for you, you could simply recognize your partner as the incredible result of billions of years of evolution.

* As you undress one another, 'worship' each part of the body that's revealed; massage it with perfumed oil.
* Alternate between staring deeply into your partner's eyes (to experience your partner's spirituality), closing your eyes (to experience your own spirituality) and gazing intensely at any object that, for you, symbolizes the universe – it could be a stone or a tree outside the window.
* The man should use the technique for multiple orgasms to prolong sex as much as possible, thus allowing the 'happy chemicals' to build to a maximum for both of you.
* Have periods with little movement; you could even break off altogether for a short while.
* As the feelings intensify, you might find it helpful to reduce bodily contact to the genitals alone, so that you can concentrate on your spiritual experience, which hopefully you will have.

The belief is that the reality of the universe can only be grasped during a state of consciousness that's different from normal consciousness. In other words, the state that can be achieved during sex. As the sadhakas (followers of tantra) say: 'Spirit alone can know spirit.'

> The modern, small-minded ascetic endeavours to grow spiritually by destroying his physical instincts instead of by using them. But I would proclaim that we are set in the world to mould matter that it may express our spirits.
>
> Marie Stopes (1880–1958),
> Scottish birth control campaigner

Breakthrough

Would you say your sex life has improved and, if so, are you happier generally?

a Yes.

b Yes, sex has improved but that doesn't make me any happier the rest of the time.

c No, we're still not having very much sex.

d No, I/we can't seem to manage these techniques.

If you answered 'a', you've made a breakthrough and can move on to Chapter 12.

If you answered 'b' because your sex life has improved but you're no happier generally, it could be you're still not having enough of the right kind of sex, or, if you're a man, it could be you're ejaculating too often. Are you having some kind of sexual activity (not necessarily intercourse) every day? As regards ejaculation, read Rule number 6 again and keep practising the technique for multiple orgasms.

If you answered 'c' because you're not having sex very often, there could be all kinds of reasons for that. Some general advice is to agree to give sex a higher priority as a trial, whether you feel like it or not. Many people, no matter how much they enjoy sex when they're doing it, don't feel a very strong drive the rest of the time (take another look at Chapter 9, especially the part about people not being very good at predicting what will make them happy). So it may be necessary to agree to have sex with a certain regularity, at least to see what happens. You don't wait until you're starving before you eat, so why should you wait until you're 'sex-starved' before you have sex?

If you answered 'd' because you and your partner are having problems with the advanced techniques, don't let that become a source of anxiety. There's no rush to perfect these techniques. Enjoy the journey.

Focus points

The main points to remember from this chapter are:

* sex makes us all happy – men and women equally – and the optimum frequency for happiness seems to be four or more times a week
* women can absorb 'happy chemicals' from semen through the walls of their vagina
* other key elements in happy sex are love, the absence of inhibition, spirituality and monogamy
* the techniques of happy sex include plenty of cuddling, self-expression, music, multiple orgasms for women and simultaneous orgasms (except in tantric sex)
* tantric sex adds spirituality and takes lovemaking to a higher plane.

Keep smiling

If love is blind, why is lingerie so popular?

Next step

Hopefully you're now practising tantric sex and enriching the spiritual dimension of your lovemaking. In Chapter 12, we're going to put the final piece of the happiness jigsaw into place. We're going to see how you can enrich all of your life by taking a more spiritual approach and especially through two very simple but vitally important techniques – kindness and gratitude.

12

Spirituality, gratitude and kindness

In this chapter you will learn:

▶ *why you're never really alone*
▶ *how nature makes you happy*
▶ *how kindness makes you happy*
▶ *how to achieve bliss through a more spiritual style of meditation.*

He who wants to do good knocks at the gate; he who loves finds the gates open.

Sir Rabindranath Tagore (1861–1941),
Bengali writer

When the power of love overcomes the love of power the world will know peace.

Jimi Hendrix (1942–70),
American rock guitarist and singer/songwriter

No matter how happy you are made by the things I've already described, there's always going to be a 'hole' if you don't include spirituality. Human beings need spirituality. Spirituality has many definitions but I'm talking about your sense of connection with other things – with people you know, with people you don't know, with animals, plants, this planet, this solar system, the furthest reaches of the universe.

Let me ask you a question. If, somehow, you could know for a fact that there were people like you living on another planet a thousand light years away, would it make any difference to you? If it would, that's spirituality. The sense that you're connected to life although no actual connection is apparent.

Two of the most famous words of the 20th century were written by the novelist E. M. Forster: 'Only connect!' We all crave it. We all fear separation. Connection is happiness.

Let's see how spiritual – how connected – you are.

Self-assessment: How spiritual am I?

For each of the following ten groups of statements choose the one that most closely reflects your view.

1

   a Money and possessions are not priorities for me.

   b Money and all the things it buys are very important to me.

2

   a I attend a place of worship regularly.

   b I have a religion but I seldom attend a place of worship.

   c I'm an atheist.

3

   a I love to be outdoors enjoying the natural world.

   b Outdoors is muddy, scratchy, infested with insects and generally overrated.

4

   a I feel a tremendous sense of connection with other people, and everything on the planet.

   b Fundamentally, we're all alone in the world.

5

   a I make a point of helping other people.

   b If someone close to me is in a fix I'll do my best to help, but you can't help everybody.

   c I look out for myself.

6

   a In my small way I try to make the world a better place for everyone.

   b It's more or less impossible to make any difference to the world and it's a waste of time trying.

7

   a There are several people I feel especially grateful to.

   b I've had to make my own way and I don't feel grateful to anybody.

8

   a I feel grateful for so many things in my life.

   b I have little or nothing to feel grateful for.

9

   a I do my best to give and receive love wherever I go.

   b Saying you love people you hardly know is pretty stupid.

10

   a I meditate regularly.

   b I sometimes sort of meditate.

   c Meditation is a load of rubbish and I would never do it.

If you answered mostly 'a', you're obviously spiritual, kind, grateful – and loved. If you answered mostly 'b' or 'c', read on to find out how 'getting connected' can significantly increase your happiness.

Key idea: Atheists can be spiritual

You don't have to be religious to be spiritual. Even the Dalai Lama, the Buddhist spiritual leader of the Tibetan people, recognizes as much. 'I believe,' he says, 'that each individual should embark upon a spiritual path that is best suited to his or her mental disposition, natural inclination, temperament, belief, family and cultural background.' In other words, you don't have to identify yourself as a Buddhist or a Christian or a member of any other religion – although, of course, you may.

All life is connected

The universe is a very strange place. As the biologist J. B. S. Haldane once observed: 'The universe is not only queerer than we suppose, it is queerer than we can suppose.' And the 'queerest' things of all are us, our dependence on everything else in the universe and our connection with them. In fact, we never can walk alone even if we want to.

I'm now going to prove this to you. I think you'll find it very difficult to be unhappy when you know these facts. You should feel exhilarated.

▶ Proof number 1

Everything, including the air, is made of atoms. Atoms mostly consist of empty space – a nucleus circled at a vast distance (in relative terms) by one or more electrons. One analogy is that if the whole atom was enlarged to the size of the dome of St Paul's Cathedral, the nucleus would only be the size of a grain of sand in the middle.

Since we're mostly empty space and everything else is mostly empty space there's far less difference than you might think between you and anything else. In other words, you're rather like a tornado in the air or a whirlpool in a river with things (nutrients, for example) constantly entering your vortex and leaving it.

Key idea: Babies feel 'oneness'

There's evidence to suggest that newborn babies can't distinguish between themselves and anything else. This leads to two interesting possibilities:

1 The idea of merging with the 'Great Oneness' is nothing more than a desire to regress to that early infantile state.

2 An infant is right to feel that sense of being at one with the universe because, actually, it is. It's we adults who have dcluded ourselves that we're separate.

▶ Proof number 2

Every single atom of which you are composed came from the stars and has already been in millions of other organisms – because atoms can survive for a million years or more. A billion may well have been in Shakespeare or Boudicca (or any other historical figure you can think of). Probably none of those atoms has been part of you for more than nine years and the vast majority won't form part of you for more than a month.

▶ Proof number 3

You have something like 10,000 trillion cells in your body and each cell has millions of components, including mitochondria, which are the cell's power stations. Way back in time mitochondria seem to have been bacteria, living quite separately, and even now they have their own DNA, quite distinct from yours. This means that, in a manner of speaking, you're not a single organism but a whole collection of bacteria living in mutual dependence.

▶ Proof number 4

In 1997, scientists at the University of Geneva succeeded in separating a pair of sub-atomic particles and sending one in one direction and the other in the opposite direction. When the particles were seven miles apart, the scientists changed the axis of one of the particles and the other particle – in accordance with the predictions of quantum theory – changed its axis instantly. No one knows how.

To scientists this means that instead of the properties of systems being determined by the properties of the individual parts (the 'classical' view of physics), the properties of the parts are determined by the whole (the 'quantum' view of physics).

To philosophers this is proof that, in the words of one Buddhist sage: 'Things derive their being and nature by mutual dependence and are nothing in themselves.' Or, in the words of the English metaphysical poet and preacher John Donne, 'No man is an island, entire of itself'.

It also means there could be some way, after all, of communicating with those people on that distant planet.

> What is now proved was once only imagin'd.
>
> William Blake (1757–1827), English poet and mystic

▶ Proof number 5

The psychologist Carl Jung noticed that certain symbols recurred throughout history in different societies all over the world, even in societies that had had no contact with one another. This, among other things, prompted him to develop the idea of the 'collective unconscious'. Inside us all are 'an untold abundance of images which have accumulated over millions of years of development'.

Try it now: Always remember the five proofs

Next time you're feeling overwhelmed by a problem, read the five proofs above. They should help you get things into perspective.

Case study: Tricia

Tricia enjoys stargazing with a pair of binoculars. This is her recipe for overcoming the blues. 'I know it sounds a bit crazy but when I'm feeling down I put on some ethereal kind of music and look at my book of photographs taken by the Hubble Space Telescope. When I see the pictures of, say, the Andromeda Galaxy or the Whirlpool Galaxy M51, I'm absolutely overwhelmed by the beauty of it all. It never fails to make me feel blissfully happy because I just can't help feeling there has to be some meaning to it.'

Say 'hello' to your very big family

As we saw in Chapter 10, the more relatives you're close to, the happier you're likely to be. Well, here's another amazing piece of 'queer' information. You've got billions of close relatives.

How? Because, according to many scientists, life on Earth began successfully only once. Think about it. It's staggering. If it's true it means – it's connection again – that every single living thing is directly related to every other living thing.

Let me elaborate. Back in the dawn of time (about 3.85 billion years ago, scientists think) there were millions of primeval ponds all over the planet, each going 'glug glug glug'. It wouldn't be unreasonable to assume that when the conditions for life to arise were right, life would have occurred in thousands of these ponds all over the planet. But no, it happened, successfully anyway, in just one of those ponds, at one moment, once only. And it never, ever, happened again.

We're all – everything that lives – descendants of the same blob out of the same glug.

If you're a religious person, you'll certainly find confirmation in this for your belief in the extraordinary probability that life successfully began on Earth only once. And that may certainly make you happy.

> Some people say there is a God; others say there is no God. The truth probably lies somewhere in between.
>
> W. B. Yeats (1865–1939), Irish poet

But even if you're an atheist, you can't fail to be moved by the knowledge that a tree is a relative of yours; go and hug one now. Your dog is a relative of yours; go and pat him. The grass is a relative of yours; go and lie on it. Both the tiniest creatures in the sea and the largest are relatives of yours; go and swim with them.

This is true even if it turns out all life didn't come from the same blob. Because we know that in any two human beings anywhere on the planet, 99.9 per cent of their genes, on average, will be identical. We share 90 per cent of our genes with mice, and 60 per cent with flies. We even share genes with vegetables. I could go on. The point is that being in contact with nature will make you happy because you're part of it.

If you live in the countryside you've got a head start. If you live in the town, especially if you don't have a garden, you'll need to make more of an effort. But wherever you live, get out and make the acquaintance of your relatives.

If that all sounds too mystical for your taste, bear this in mind. Human beings have been on the planet (depending on what you call a human being) for about 15 million years. And 99.9 per cent of that time has been spent living 'in nature'. Nowadays, most of us live in towns but human beings didn't evolve to live in towns. Our way of living, our environment, has changed very fast but we haven't changed at all. And we can't change. At least, not that quickly.

You're almost certainly living in a town. Most people are. And you may say you like it, even love it. Tried the countryside and couldn't stand it. Couldn't abide the mud. But then, why are you reading this book? I'll tell you why. Because there's a little void inside you that you can't ever seem to fill up. Am I right? And now you know one of the reasons.

Remember this: Your garden is your savannah

The savannah, where humans lived for 2 million years, is imprinted in you. It's in your genes. That's why we all try to recreate the savannah in our gardens – open grassland, a few trees, a water feature. Fight it if you insist, but that's not the way to happiness.

Try it now: Back to nature

Go out into the countryside and search for a landscape that 'speaks' to you. A place that seems special. Then don't just look at it. Get in it – smell things, taste things, touch things, hug them. Get down on your hands and knees. Roll on the ground. If it's practical, take your clothes off – at least some of them. Get skin contact. Open your arms like a bird and 'glide' around. If there's water, swim naked. Feel how much you're a part of nature and how right it is.

NO NOISE ON THE SAVANNAH

There was little noise on the savannah. And when there was, it meant just one thing: danger! It still means the same to you today, even though you may not realize it. It's just one example of nature inside you and the very physical effects of ignoring it.

You may think you're used to the noise of the city. But your body thinks otherwise. Tests on people who have lived in towns for years show they're still stressed by noise. Even when you're asleep at night your body is aware of noise. Occasional noise at night may mean nothing worse than fatigue in the morning. But years of noise mean:

- ▶ higher levels of stress hormones in the blood, including cortisol

- ▶ higher levels of glucose, insulin, lipids and cholesterol in the blood

- ▶ higher loss of magnesium from cells

- increased heartbeat

- increased blood pressure

- decreased blood circulation to peripheral organs

- weakened immune system

- greater susceptibility to psychological problems.

It's been calculated that an increased risk of damage to health begins at night-time noise levels as low as 42 decibels (dB). At around 55 dB you have a 5 per cent increased probability of ill health, and at 70 dB the probability goes up to more than 11 per cent. These levels are not very loud; a nearby jackhammer, for example, would be 90 dB.

Noise is only one aspect of city life that undermines happiness. Others include the overcrowding, the pushing and shoving, that – paradoxically – leads to alienation from other people: the very opposite of the connection we're all trying to feel.

Try it now: Practical noise-reduction

Review your lifestyle and living conditions to see if there are ways of reducing noise. Perhaps you could install double-glazing, for example.

Altruism equals happiness

So I've proved to you that you're connected. So what? Well, apart from making you less likely to feel lonely, connection motivates you towards the happy state of altruism.

According to research carried out for the volunteering charity CSV:

- 37 per cent of respondents feel happier when they do something to help the environment or wildlife

- 55 per cent of respondents feel happier when helping a neighbour or friend (the figure is 67 per cent for the over 65s)

- 63 per cent of respondents say volunteering helps them feel less stressed.

And here's an unexpected bonus; 17 per cent of respondents said volunteering improved their sex lives!

It's not solely a question of feeling good about yourself and what you're achieving. It's also a question of taking control of your own life. When we do nothing, we feel as if we're victims of outside forces which are, for example, destroying the rainforests, causing the extinction of whales or bombing children. When we do something about it we feel more at peace with ourselves.

Key idea: Variety is the spice

In one series of experiments, participants who performed a variety of kind acts registered a significant increase in happiness. But kindness is as subject to 'hedonic adaptation' as anything else. Those who kept repeating the same kind acts soon showed no increase in happiness. The message is: employ variety in this, as in most other things to do with happiness.

Remember this: Small is beautiful

You don't have to tackle a huge project. Research by Jennifer Aaker, Melanie Rudd and Michael I. Norton demonstrated that it's easier to make other people, and yourself, happier when you do something small that has a high chance of success. Just trying to make other people smile was extremely effective.

Try it now: Kindness day

Designate one day of the week as 'kindness day'. On that day perform at least five different acts of kindness that you wouldn't otherwise have done. In other words, these have to be rather special and unusual acts. Here are some ideas.

✳ Call a lonely relative or friend you haven't spoken to for a while and have a nice chat.

✳ Clear up some rubbish in a public place.

✳ Send a donation to charity.

* If a friend, colleague or acquaintance seems a bit down, find out why and try to help.
* Give a friend, colleague or acquaintance a break by offering to spend an evening babysitting or looking after an elderly person.
* When you're going shopping, see if you can buy anything for a neighbour or friend.
* Take on a chore you wouldn't normally do.
* Give a hand to someone who's struggling to do something.
* Sign an online petition aimed at making the world a better place.
* Bring all your immediate work colleagues some special pastries for the coffee break.

Remember this: Help others help yourself

The person you're really being kind to is yourself because you're going to be much happier.

Case study: Richard

Only a year before I met him, Richard (whom we encountered in Chapter 9) had tried to commit suicide. Very early one morning he'd ridden his motorbike flat out down a dangerously winding road and deliberately let go of the handlebars. Nothing happened. That experience convinced him that every life has a point. He believes he didn't die because he was destined to use his experience with horses to help people. He believes that's the purpose of his existence. And he's happy.

> I don't know what your destiny will be, but one thing I know: the only ones among you who will be really happy are those who have sought and found how to serve.
> Albert Schweitzer (1875–1965),
> German-French missionary surgeon

Two researchers (Emmons and McCullough, 2003) have found that it's not only being kind to others that brings happiness, but also feeling grateful for the kind things others do for you – and simply for being alive on planet Earth. In one of their studies, participants were asked to keep diaries detailing their general attitudes, moods and physical health. They were then divided into three groups. Each week:

- **group 1** was asked to write down five things that had happened to them for which they felt grateful.

- **group 2** was asked to write down five things that had happened to them about which they felt aggrieved.

- **group 3** was asked to write down any five events that had happened to them.

At the end of the study period, those in the 'gratitude group' were 25 per cent happier than they had been – they were more optimistic about the future, felt better about their lives and had begun taking almost 1.5 hours more exercise than the other two groups (which itself would have made a further contribution to their happiness).

In a further experiment, the two researchers worked with adults who suffered disabilities and demonstrated that by developing an attitude of gratitude for the things they *could* do, the participants became more satisfied with their lives, more optimistic and slept better (a general indicator of happiness and well-being).

Remember this: Take nothing for granted

We all tend to take for granted the things that we're used to. In terms of happiness, that's a very big mistake.

Try it now: Make 'gratitude time'

✳ Spend a couple of minutes thinking of things you feel grateful for. If you don't feel grateful because you believe you've achieved everything on your own, try imagining a world without sunshine, sunsets, sea to swim in, beaches, trees, flowers, birds... Then imagine life without friends and people who love you. Just two minutes a week of 'gratitude exercise' is all it takes for most people to feel happier. Other people find the gratitude exercise more effective if it's done every day for one week every three months. Experiment to see what frequency works best for you.

✼ Here's an exercise that combines both gratitude and kindness. Think of someone who has had an important and positive impact on your life, for example, a school teacher, a mentor, someone who taught you a skill as an adult or someone who helped you up the career ladder. Write down why you feel grateful to that person. Then phone them and say you want to meet. If they ask why, say it's a secret but a nice one. Once you're face to face with that person (and, perhaps, their partner or family) either read out what you've written or run through it from memory, whichever feels most comfortable. Probably it will all get a bit emotional, but everyone involved is going to feel very happy afterwards.

Hatred paralyses life; love releases it. Hatred confuses life; love harmonizes it. Hatred darkens life; love illumines it.
Martin Luther King, Jr. (1929–68),
American civil rights campaigner

Meditation and spirituality

We've talked about getting out into nature and experiencing the connection. There is another way. In Chapter 7 we looked at meditation. I said then that your reservoir of inner happiness was refilled by your spiritual connection with everything. Now that you've read the 'proofs' I've given above, you'll know that this isn't just a fanciful way of talking. When you reach down into yourself in meditation, you're actually reaching out into… what do you prefer to call it? You could say nature, you could say the Great Oneness, you could say the Divine Consciousness. I'll leave it up to you.

1 Sitting or lying down with your eyes closed, notice your breathing.

2 Without forcing anything, gradually slow down your breathing.

3 Make your exhalations longer than your inhalations.

4 Empty your mind of any thoughts of past or future.

5 Concentrate on experiencing the present moment that is your breath.

6 If any thoughts push their way into your mind, let them drift past; don't pursue them.

7 When your breathing is slow and relaxed, notice your heartbeat.

8 Without forcing anything, gradually try to think your heartbeat slower.

9 Next, notice the sound of your blood in your ears.

10 Without forcing anything, gradually try to think the sound slower.

11 In the same way, visit any other parts of your body that you choose.

12 Now notice the little dots that 'illuminate' the blackness of your closed eyes.

13 Imagine the dots are stars and that you're floating in space.

14 Relax your jaw and let your mouth open into a smile.

15 What is it that keeps you afloat in space? It is love. You have nothing to fear; love is everywhere, within and without.

16 You are in a state of bliss.

Breakthrough

Are you:

a feeling more spiritual

b practising more kindness

c feeling more grateful.

If you answered 'yes' to all three questions, you've made a major breakthrough. If you answered 'no' to any or all questions, read through the five proofs again, continue with the 'kindness days' and work on developing your feelings of gratitude. Remember, all of these things have been proven experimentally to make people happier. They're not merely politically correct ideas. They actually do work.

Focus points

The main points to remember from this chapter are:

* separation equals unhappiness; connection equals happiness
* the atoms in your body came from the stars and have previously been in other people
* showing kindness to others will bring happiness to you
* by learning to be grateful you'll also learn to be happy
* humans developed in the natural world – you can't be happy if you're cut off from it.

Keep smiling

> The greatest pleasure I know, is to do a good action by stealth, and to have it found out by accident.
>
> Charles Lamb (1775–1834), English essayist

Next step

You've now learned a huge range of techniques for increasing your personal happiness. You've learned how to combat negative thoughts and also how to accept them, how to overcome harmful emotions, the importance of exercise and good nutrition, how to be yourself and do what you want to do, why variety is essential, how to improve your relationships, and the role of spirituality, kindness and gratitude. In Chapter 13, you'll learn how all of these elements can be combined into a one-week programme guaranteed to make you happier.

13

Your seven-day happiness plan

In this chapter you will learn:

▶ *how seven days can change your life.*

> Whatever you can do or dream you can, begin it now.
> Boldness has genius, power and magic in it...
>
> Goethe (1749–1832), German poet

For the next seven days, conduct your life in accordance with the following ten principles. While you're doing it, remember to keep that 'happiness diary' described in Chapter 1. That way you'll be able to keep track of the things that work best for you.

▶ 1 Start the day right

For happiness you need 7–8 hours sleep, and you don't want to get up abruptly as this tends to make people irritable. If you possibly can, lie in bed a while before getting up.

While you're contemplating the day ahead, smile. And keep on smiling. By doing so you can 'hijack' your body's chemistry. You can smile to make yourself happy, rather than the other way around.

The next thing to do after your first in-bed smile is cuddle. If someone is in bed with you, cuddle them. Aim to cuddle everyone in the household. If you live alone, cuddle your pet. If you don't have a pet, cuddle yourself. Carry on cuddling at every opportunity during the day.

▶ 2 Be positive

The single most important thing you can do to increase your happiness is to decide to be happy. Without a conscious effort you will not improve your 'baseline' level. Remember, it's morally right to be happy (see Chapter 1).

Spend some of that time in bed prioritizing for the day ahead. Don't think in terms of things you 'should' do, or money or status or anything like that. Prioritize instead in terms of the things that give you 'the maximum satisfaction of your whole being' (see Chapter 9). Aim to maximize the pleasure you get from each thing by giving it your full attention. Make sure you don't go to sleep each night without having had an experience that makes the day distinct and gives it a value.

Also, make plans for all the wonderful things you're going to do in the coming weeks, months and years. Write them down. Organize them. Look forward to them.

▶ 3 No negatives

During this week you're not allowed to complain about anything or criticize anything or anyone in any way at all. So, no scowling, no sighing and no raised eyebrows. It certainly isn't easy (see Chapter 2) but it's a fascinating exercise. It will, firstly, make you realize how much you complain and criticize, and secondly, teach you to find more positive ways of communicating. Oh, and you're not allowed to criticize yourself.

No negative emotions either. Every day, forgive somebody for the bad things you consider he/she has done to you. Let go of all negative emotions by empathizing (see Chapter 3). Defuse tense situations with laughter. (Practise by reading funny books, watching funny films and swapping jokes with friends.)

Eradicate all cravings for those expensive things you can't afford. Longing for them is only making you unhappy. Forget about them (see Chapter 2).

Don't go comparing your partner, your friends or relatives, your possessions or your situation with those you consider to be 'better'. Instead, make comparisons with people who are 'worse off'.

▶ 4 Introduce variety

Because of what the psychologists call 'hedonic adaptation', we all need variety in our lives. No matter how pleasurable something is at first, we derive less pleasure from it the more often we do it. So every day this week, firstly, do something entirely new, and secondly, find a new way of doing things that have become routine. Don't think only in terms of 'big' things. 'Little' things can generate just as much happiness, and they're usually accessible and affordable. For example, go to work by a different route, try a food that's new to you, discover a new author, make love in a new position. But also aim to do at least one 'big' thing during the week, something you've always wanted to do but never have (see Chapter 9). We all need to have the sense that we're progressing, that we're heading somewhere. That 'in every day, in every way, I'm getting better and better'. So learn something new as well. It could be to do with your job, it could be to do with your partner, it could be the name of a star in the sky or a tree in the garden. Doing new things may mean overcoming your inhibitions, by doing the very thing you're anxious about. If there's a particularly difficult one, break it down into several stages and tackle one stage each day.

▶ 5 Express yourself

Let the real you be apparent in everything you do. Be creative. Start with your appearance and then move on to every aspect of your life. No longer feel you have to hide the way you really are, the way you really feel, or the things you want to do. If you have a partner, try tentatively swapping fantasies.

▶ 6 Play with your mind

When you have the opportunity (perhaps on the train or bus to work), spend time visualizing happy things – either memories or future events. Manipulate the submodalities (Chapter 6) to make the sensation of happiness more intense.

Set aside some time for a session of self-hypnosis. State as your aim: 'I am entering into a state of self-hypnosis so that I can hand over to my unconscious mind the task of making me feel happier.' Then in the second part of the process (Step 5f/g, see Chapter 6), visualize a happy scene you'd like to come true.

Whenever you have anxious, sad or negative thoughts this week, practise saying to yourself: 'I am having the thought that...'. Then step away from it.

Write about your values as described in Chapter 8, and resolve to live in accordance with them.

▶ 7 Play with your body

Eat plenty of 'happy foods'. But don't try to convert to 'happy eating' all in one go; the body needs time to adjust and it can't be accomplished in one week (Chapter 4).

If you haven't yet begun an exercise programme, get started this week. Take a look at Chapter 5 for ideas on the best way to go about it. You won't be able to get the full benefits in a week but you should get a taste of the pleasure to come.

Cultivate your sensuality – your body is the tool your mind uses to explore the world. When you eat, really focus on the food; savour it; notice the different tastes. When you walk, notice how your body revels in the movement and how your skin relishes the breeze. When you shower, enjoy soaping every part of your body. For at least an hour listen to music that makes you feel good – don't, for this week, listen to anything that makes you feel sad, however great it might be.

▶ 8 Improve your relationships

Get that oxytocin going (see Chapter 10) by being more tactile (although only when it's appropriate). When you shake hands, really feel the hand. Hug. When someone needs support, put an arm round their shoulders. Massage someone close to you and have them give you a massage.

Tell everyone close to you that you love them. Say these words a minimum of five times every day. Empathize.

If you have a partner, bathe or shower together, sleep naked together, massage one another, brush one another's hair, eat food from one another's lips and reveal 'secret' thoughts. Have sex at least four times during the week. Aim to make it as tantric as possible.

If you don't have a partner, spend time with friends or relatives, talking intimately. The idea is to break down that sense of separateness and put an end to that feeling of being alone. Enjoy practising multiple orgasm techniques on your own (see Chapter 11).

▶ 9 Get connected

Get out into nature and say hello to your relatives. Don't just admire the view as a spectator; get right in it. Feel the connection (see Chapter 12).

I'm not going to rush you into getting a pet because it might not be appropriate in your present circumstances. But you need to find a way of interacting with an animal or animals. Maybe you can play with the neighbour's dog, take a riding lesson or help at an animal rescue centre.

Spend at least 20 minutes every day on meditation (see Chapter 7).

Take the time to stare up at the night sky, enjoy its beauty and reflect on what an incredible place the universe is (see Chapter 12).

Make one day a 'kindness day' (see Chapter 12) and perform five different acts of kindness you wouldn't normally have done. Make one an act of generosity for a stranger or strangers, without thought of recognition. You could, for example, give money – what you can afford – to a charity. Take time over choosing it. Savour the impact your donation is going to have. And you could give time to charity work (an especially good idea if you're feeling lonely).

Make another day 'gratitude day' and think of things to be grateful for. You don't have to try to feel grateful to other people if you don't want (some people find that very difficult), but you can certainly feel grateful for all the delightful things about living on planet Earth. Show an interest in everything (which ties in rather nicely with the importance of variety – see point 4 above). Stop to take a look at those flowers. What are their names? How many petals do they have? Where has that bird migrated from? Why is the sky blue on a sunny day? Which planet is that bright object in the sky? You'll never stop being amazed at how wonderful the world is.

▶ 10 Review the day

Just before you go to sleep, replay the day in your mind and note the things you did well and the things you didn't do so well. Don't view it as self-criticism. Simply take note of the day's events and your response to them. Where things didn't go so well, try to work out why and see if you can devise a better way for next time. Where they did go well, congratulate yourself. Look forward to the next day with optimism. As you drift off to sleep tell yourself this, 'When I wake up tomorrow morning I will feel very, very happy!'

How happy are you now?

Have you completed your seven-day happiness plan? If so, is your new score in the questionnaire in Chapter 1 higher than when you started this book?

1 Yes, I'm happier.

2 I've completed the plan but, no, I don't feel any happier.

3 No, I haven't followed the plan.

Hopefully you answered '1'. If you answered '2', are you sure you've really completed the plan and followed all the practical steps described in the book? (If so, your lack of response suggests you might be suffering from depression, in which case you should consult your GP.) If you answered '3' because you haven't followed the plan at all or haven't followed it properly, read through it again and implement it. There are no exams and no certificates but there is a prize – your happiness.

Finally, I leave you with one more quote. These five words of Gandhi's should be the basis on which you live your life. Your very, very happy life.

My life is my message.

Mohandas K. Gandhi (1869–1948),
Indian nationalist leader and pacifist

Bibliography

Books

Argyle, M. (2001). *The Psychology of Happiness*. London: Routledge.

Bloom, W. (2011). *The Endorphin Effect*. London: Piatkus.

Burns, D. D. (2008). *Feeling Good: The New Mood Therapy*. New York: Avon.

Carper, J. (2000). *The Food Pharmacy*. London: Simon & Schuster.

Chang, J. (1977). *The Tao of Love and Sex*. London: Wildwood House Ltd.

Chia, M. & Abrams Arava, D. (2002). *The Multi-Orgasmic Man*. London: Thorsons.

Chia, M., Chia, M., Abrams, D. & Abrams, R. C. (2001). *The Multi-Orgasmic Couple*. London: Thorsons.

Craze, R. (2002). *Teach Yourself Tantric Sex*. London: Teach Yourself.

H. H. Dalai Lama & Cutler, H. (1999). *The Art of Happiness*. London: Coronet.

Diener, E. & Biswas-Diener, R. (2008). *Happiness: Unlocking the Mysteries of Psychological Wealth*. Oxford: Wiley Blackwell.

Fromm, E. (1995). *The Art of Loving*. London: Thorsons.

Gilbert, D. (2006). *Stumbling on Happiness*. London: HarperPress.

Goleman, D. (1996). *Emotional Intelligence*. London: Bloomsbury.

Gray, J. (2002) *Men are from Mars, Women are from Venus*. London: Thorsons.

Haidt, J. (2006). *The Happiness Hypothesis*. London: William Heinemann.

Harris, R. (2008). *The Happiness Trap*. London: Robinson.

Jenner, P. (2007). *Beat Your Depression*. London: Hodder Arnold.

Jenner, P. (2006). *Teach Yourself Great Sex*. London: Hodder Education.

Jenner, P. (2007). *Teach Yourself Kama Sutra*. London: Hodder.

Klein, S. (2015). *The Science of Happiness*. New York: Scribe.

Layard, R. (2011). *Happiness: Lessons from a New Science*. London: Penguin.

Lyubomirsky, S. (2010). *The How of Happiness*. London: Piatkus.

McMahon, D. (2006). *The Pursuit of Happiness*. London: Allen Lane.

Mumford, S. (2006). *The New Complete Guide to Massage*. London: Hamlyn.

Nettle, D. (2006). *Happiness: The Science Behind Your Smile*. Oxford: OUP.

Ozaniec, N. (2007). *Teach Yourself Meditation*. London: Teach Yourself.

Reed Gach, M. (1997). *Intimate Touch*. London: Piatkus.

Riskin, M. & Banker-Riskin, A. (1997). *Simultaneous Orgasm and Other Joys of Sexual Intimacy*. Alameda: Hunter House.

Stewart, N. (2010). *The Complete Body Massage Course*. London: Collins & Brown.

Tannen, D. (2007). *You Just Don't Understand*. New York: William Morrow.

Walsh, A. (1996). *The Science of Love*. Buffalo: Prometheus Books.

Whichello Brown, D. (2010). *Get Started in Massage*. London: Teach Yourself.

Websites

(Retrieved April 2015)

Website of Dr Martin Seligman, founder of 'positive psychology': https://www.authentichappiness.sas.upenn.edu

Website of the Positive Psychology Center: www.positivepsychology.org

Advice on how to forgive: www.theforgivenessproject.com

Advice on how to pursue happiness through education: www.pursuit-of-happiness.org

Tips on how to avoid stress and how to cope with it: www.stressinstitute.com

Website of Action For Happiness, an international movement for positive social change: www.actionforhappiness.org

Website of the Greater Good Science Center, which investigates 'the science of a meaningful life': http://greatergood.berkeley.edu

Website of Daniel Gilbert, author of *Stumbling on Happiness*: www.stumblingonhappiness.com

Website of Paul Jenner, author of this book: www.pauljenner.eu

Website of Stefan Klein, author of *The Science of Happiness*: www.stefanklein.info/en

Data on various aspects of happiness all over the world: http://worlddatabaseofhappiness.eur.nl/hap_cor/cor_fp.htm

Index